Thinking for a Living:
The Coming Age of Knowledge Work

Kenneth A. Megill

Thinking for a Living:
The Coming Age of
Knowledge Work

K·G·Saur München 2004

Bibliographic information published by Die Deutsche Bibliothek
Die Deutsche Bibliothek lists this publication in the Deutsche Nationalbibliografie;
detailed bibliographic data is available in the internet at http://dnb.ddb.de.

Printed on acid-free paper

© 2004 K. G. Saur Verlag GmbH, München

Typesetting by Florence Production Ltd., Stoodleigh, Devon, Great Britain.

Printed and bound by Strauss GmbH, Mörlenbach, Germany.

ISBN 3-598-11638-1

In Memory of

Alice Gannon

A knowledge worker who told her boss: "I'll give you an idea worth a million dollars every year or two. Your job is to pay me in the meantime."

Rest in Peace, Alice

The Authors

Ken Megill is a transformer of organizations and people. He is a published professional philosopher and teacher and a forty year member of the American Philosophical Association. He spent his last twenty years in the practical pursuit of knowledge management. He is a certified records manager, a certified archivist and holds a master of library and information science degree. He has been an organizer and president of the trade union representing 8,000 faculty and professional employees in Florida. His previous books include a consideration of how corporate memory can be preserved in the electronic age, a discussion of the management of a large number of documents, a handbook on managing information for government agencies, and a book on democratic political theory.

Terry Balven was responsible for the Appendix. He is currently working for the Assistant Secretary of the Air Force for Acquisition to establish the position of chief information officer for the acquisition community. His charter is to build an organization and methodology to organize and direct an array of improvement initiatives associated with information, knowledge, and their uses. The goal is to align process change, investments in information technology, and change in how people think about work in order to deliver transformational improvement in how the Air Force and Department of Defense acquire weapon systems. He served thirty years in the United States Air Force, retiring as a colonel after a wide variety of operational and staff assignments. Colonel Balven directed the integrated digital environment project for the United States Air Force, which was led by Ken Megill.

Contents

Work

"Tom said to himself that it was not such a hollow world after all . . . . If he had been a great and wise philosopher, like the writer of this book, he would now have comprehended that Work consists of whatever a body is obliged to do and that Play consists of whatever a body is not obliged to do."

Mark Twain. The Adventures of Tom Sawyer. Chapter II: "The Glorious Whitewasher."

Knowledge

"But how is it that some people enjoy spending a great deal of time in my company . . . It is because they enjoy hearing me examine those who think that they are wise when they are not – an experience which has its amusing side."

Socrates, Apology (19c)

Acknowledgements

This book is dedicated to the memory of Alice Gannon, a wonderful records manager. We shared a minimalist view of our profession – we agreed we should keep as little as possible, but all of the right things, we should have as few staff as possible, and pay them very well, and we should automate every conceivable task.

At our last lunch together – shortly before she finally lost her battle with an illness that would have felled most of us years ago – she asked me what I was up to. When I told her I was thinking of writing a book with the title, "Thinking for a Living," she said, "I know what that means." She went to say, "I tell my boss that I will come up with an idea to save him a million dollars or so every year or so. In the meantime, I expect him to pay me." Alice was worth every penny she was paid – and I miss having lunch with her.

Thanks go to the many people who endured my exposition of thoughts and ideas that eventually made it into this book. Some who read the manuscript as it developed include Clare Imholtz, Marilyn Barth and Deb Marshall, three former students and colleagues. These three read a much earlier version of this book and told me to start over. I did . . . and what is here is hopefully better for their honest and brutal (although nicely said) advice. They even had the stamina to come back and read this later version and have said that it is all right if I send it off to the publisher.

Barry Wheeler, my colleague and friend for many years now, made me emphasize that work, if it is thinking work, can only be done for a living if someone else finds it of value. His engineering mind-set managed to wipe out some, but surely not all, of the sections that caused him to say, "I think Rosie Scenario has stepped in." But then, from my perspective, Barry has always had a much rosier scenario than I have about where this world may be going.

The three years I spent working with the United States Air Force Integrated Digital Environment Project provided the sandbox to play in where I tried out some of my ideas on how to preserve the corporate memory of an organization – and in the process came to the conclusion that managing information is as much about changing work culture as it is about better technologies. Terry Balven, who wrote the appendix for this book, represented the Air Force in this project and provided me the space and encouragement to let my mind go. His constant question, "So if what you say is true, what do we do on Monday morning?" provided a backdrop for all of our work.

I met many wonderful people of all ranks during this project. They are, as the saying goes, too numerous to mention. During my first visit to an Air Force facility – Hanscomb Air Force Base outside Boston, I encountered Harry Pape and we worked closely together throughout the project. Many of the ideas about the importance and possibility to work in the web came from Harry. My early visits to Kirkland Air Force Base in Albuquerque allowed me to work with some very creative persons, including a person I consider a model librarian, Marsha Dreier. The folks at Kirkland struggled with (and sometimes conquered) the task of bringing knowledge management to the Air Force Research Laboratories, said to be the largest research lab in the world. Warner-Robins Air Force Base south of Macon, Georgia, was the place where I got to see, up front and close, the awesome use of technology to manage fleets of complicated flying machines.

My description of the airplane mechanic as a knowledge worker came directly from my visits there. Many people at the sprawling Wright-Patterson Air Force Base in Dayton received me with courtesy and opened up their offices and work places. Visits to the Space Center in Los Angeles, the Centers at Edwards Air Force Base in California and Eglin Air Force Base in Florida, and Arnold Air Force Base in Tennessee showed me another whole side of the complex world of applying science to making things. At the Logistics Centers in Oklahoma City and Ogden, Utah I was able to test and confirm my conclusions from Warner-Robins.

I came to what the Air Force calls its acquisition and sustainment community as an outsider and, I am sure, was often regarded as somewhat of a curiosity. The professionalism of those I worked with and their desire to do the best possible job was admirable. In the end, I admired those in the professional military environment, without altering many of my political views that I learned from my pacifist father. During many of the early visits to the facilities, I was accompanied by Major (now Lt. Colonel) Bill Richards, who wore the "Blue Suit" that gave me access to the Air Force world. As we traveled around the country and sat through many frustrating and some enlightening meetings, my respect and dedication for the working Air Force officer mounted. I met Colonel Roc Myers toward the end of the project, but found the insightful research paper he wrote as a Harvard research fellow on Knowledge Marshalling one of the best bits of thought about knowledge management.

And of course, I must mention Andy Nodine who was the last person at Kelly Air Force Base when it closed. I watched him lead the Test Equipment Center over a two year period as they struggled with the practical issues of how to capture a corporate memory and move it to another place. In the meantime, he played a central role in the development of our understanding of a work culture and how it can be transformed. Some of his analysis and advice is contained in Terry Balven's appendix.

In addition to the military professionals, I was able to work with many civilian employees and contractors who provide varied and valuable service to the community. John Rosenfeld introduced me to San Antonio – the real San Antonio – in our tour of local eateries following days of working together. I was able to see over a period of time, how he built a wonderful work environment in conditions that would only depress most people.

I was fortunate to gather some creative and innovative staff to work on the project. Dave Burnett, who then worked at Dynamics Research Corporation, took a chance by hiring me. Dave introduced me into what was a new world for me and encouraged me to give honest advice. Bob Nawrocki, a leader in the field of records management, and Mary Beth Clarkson, became colleagues on the first IDE team where we worked to invent, sometimes with patience and sometimes with exasperation, a new work culture. Dean Harris, who had been one of my students, in his quiet way made some of the very best observations and analyses of the work situation. Anthony Adamson showed me the practical side of work process reengineering as well as hours of discussion that helped me shape many of the ideas found in this book. Betsy Woods was a regular lunch companion who helped me work my way through the new world I was in. Guy St. Clair played an important role in his six months with the project as we transferred our focus to work culture transformation.

Herb Schantz, the colleague who wrote the Document Management book with me, continues to be one of my closest professional colleague and friend and I was pleased to be able to bring him into the project. We collaborated closely on everything produced by the project and it is impossible to tell which ideas are mine and which are his – except that he thinks like an engineer and I think like a philosopher.

Noel Dickover has introduced me to the concept of Performance Centered Learning Modules and provided many hours of insightful discussion. I look forward to working with him to bring his excellent work to a broader audience.

In addition to giving comments on my manuscript, Charlie Montague, Bill Larsen, and Susan Brown have been helpful by giving me a chance to think through what may be my next career – developing a business where people pay for knowledge work as a product and creating the kind of work culture that will further that work.

John Hodge, a philosopher and friend for many years noticed some obvious errors in the manuscript and gave me many suggestions that may grow into the next book. Rebecca Weiner brought the perspective of an accomplished writer and a business consultant – as well as her friendship and support.

Two other friends, Roger McFadden and Gail Gouvea served as my "general" readers and made helpful comments and suggestions.

Evie Lotze joined the Air Force team as we began to develop the Work Culture Transformation Board. We worked together over the past two years as we brought our two, companion, books to the light of day. It is an honor to be published by the same house and at the same time. Do read her book, Work Culture Transformation.

To my partner of nearly twenty years, Lawrence Tan, I cannot say how much it means that he gave me the personal space to be able to follow my ideas wherever they lead.

And, finally, thanks go to the editor, Geraldine Turpie, for encouraging me to publish this book and for welcoming us to her home near London to bring thoughts to a page. She is a true professional who thinks for a living.

Introduction

Thinking for a living. More and more of us are paid to think.

Men and women have always thought.

Until now, few have had the luxury of being paid to think.

This book is mostly about work – a particular kind of work that requires thinking. So a few words at the beginning about thought and what it is will put us on the road to understanding knowledge work.

Thinking involves language. When we think we articulate and make explicit what we take for granted. In knowledge management, what we take for granted is called tacit knowledge. Thinking is done for a purpose – to get something done, to do work.

Knowledge and Management

This book is not only about work . . . it is about knowledge and how it is managed. In that sense, it is a book on knowledge management, with the term used, we hope, in all of its richness.

Knowledge management means at least four different things to the growing number of professions trying to get a handle on the emerging new kind of work:

Librarians, records managers and archivists – those who make up the information services professions[1] generally use the term knowledge management more or less synonymously with information management – the acquisition, storage, arrangement, retrieval and use of information. Information management, for these fields, deals with managing data in a context and focuses on the content of documents. These fields also understand the importance of a "body of knowledge" – a term used by settled sciences, like physics and chemistry, and professions, like medicine and law, to refer to the knowledge associated with their profession. Knowledge management, according to this view, is what information professionals have always done – it focuses on the content of information. It is not about technology, but about content.

Engineers and information technology professionals, on the other hand, see knowledge management as a technology which develops and delivers knowledge management systems. These systems are technologies, generally software, that enable an organization to use information more extensively by using data mining, collaborative tools and telecommunications. Web technologies give us new and exciting ways to manage information more robustly.[2] The information technologists also focus on what some call an integrated digital environment – the technical environment necessary to make full use of the advances in communications and computer technology.

Both of these two groups – the IT and information service professionals see an important part of the picture. They are correct, as far as they go. However, in their literature and in their practice they make the mistake of using information management and knowledge management more or less interchangeably. We think that managing information and managing knowledge are two profoundly different activities.

Knowledge requires judgment. As we shall see, a knowledge statement is an answer to the question – "Is it a good idea to . . . ?" Knowledge management cannot be automated since it requires discernment, judgment and decision making. What are often now called "knowledge management" systems are increasingly efficient and robust information

---

[1] Guy St. Clair has written extensively about the information service professions. His most recent book calls these professions "knowledge services." His definition of information management as being concerned with the "acquisition, arrangement, storage, retrieval and use of information to produce knowledge" is fairly standard. Guy St. Clair. Beyond Degrees. Professional Learning for Knowledge Services. Munich: K.G. Saur, 2003, p. 14.

[2] Perhaps the magazine KM World (formerly known as Image Management) and the conferences it sponsors best convey this view of knowledge management.

management systems. Managing knowledge is qualitatively different from managing information.

Most knowledge management, in its current (early) incarnation, is really a kind of forms management . . . taking information/data and comparing it, contrasting, checking, and capturing it in an information system.

"Knowledge management" in this sense should probably be called information management. This form of "knowledge management" uses technologies such as data mining to identify patterns in large quantities of previously unrelated data Finding patterns is an important part of information management, but patterns alone do not give us knowledge.

Anthropologists and learning theorists, a third group, approach the topic of knowledge management from a different perspective. They focus on learning how workers acquire knowledge. They focus on the community of practice,[3] one of the key concepts that enables us to understand the nature of knowledge work. A related notion, that of the learning organization,[4] focuses on the importance of on-going learning that replaces traditional training.

Management theorists, a fourth group, talk about knowledge management from the world of management theory. Peter Drucker introduced the notion of the knowledge worker more than two decades ago. Some of the best work on the impact on management is by Ijuitsu Nonaka, the Japanese theorist who brought the term "ba" to the discussion of business theory and practice. The business theorists also speak of the importance in making the tacit knowledge of an organization explicit and developing ways to capture the tacit knowledge of an organization.

Each of these four views is important and I hope to encompass and integrate all of them in the following chapters. These professions and disciplines bring new concepts, such as integrated digital environment, knowledge work, and communities of practice that help us to understand and conceptualize the transformation in work that is underway

The immediate impetus for me to write this book came from a three-year project I led to create an integrated digital environment for the United States Air Force. Terry Balven, a wonderful military professional, provided the direction for the Air Force and writes about that project in an appendix to this book. Colonel Balven and I came from two totally

---

[3] Jean Lave is credited with being the inventor of the phrase "community of practice." See Seth Chaiklin and Jean Lave (ed), Understanding Practice. Perspectives on Activity and Context. Cambridge: Cambridge University Press, 1993.

[4] Popularized by Peter Senge, The Fifth Discipline: The Art and the Practice of the Learning Organization. New York: Doubleday/Currency, 1990.

different worlds – but as sometimes happens when cultures from different professions and bodies of knowledge overlap an environment for great creativity can emerge. We did some wonderful things together as we tried to figure out how technology can best be used to create a new environment for work.

After ending my participation in that project, I invited some of my colleagues to write about what we learned and had come to know. One of these, Evie Lotze, has written a wonderful companion book to this one called, *Work Culture Transformation*. She looks at the problem of work transformation from the world of psychology and myth. As she points out, the left side of my brain is particularly active as I struggle to make logic and sense out of our world – a task she prefers to undertake using the tools of myth and fairy tales. I end this book by pointing you to hers.

When I was freed from the day-to-day demands of the project, I was able to delve into the literature of business and management theorists, the anthropologists and learning theorists and the technologists who speak of knowledge management and the knowledge age.

When I tried to make sense out of these disparate, yet related, views, I returned to my original discipline, philosophy, and to my experiences over the years seeking to transform organizations and the social order. Philosophers know what knowledge is . . . something which seems to baffle most of those who write about knowledge management and do not use the term "knowledge" with much rigor.

For more than two thousand years knowledge has been understood as "justified true belief." Philosophers have a whole field called epistemology – the theory of knowledge. Even though there are many unresolved questions in that field, the definition and understanding of what knowledge is remains fairly constant. Knowledge has to do with judgments that we make based on evidence . . . and if we believe that we know something we also assert that what we know is true and we have evidence for its truth.

"Managing" knowledge does not make much sense if we use the philosophical definition of knowledge – for it is not possible to "manage" beliefs. In the course of the Air Force project, we found ourselves saying that "My knowledge is information for you." This formulation enables us to see the relationship between knowledge and information – for information management has to do with making the content of a body of knowledge accessible for those who need it to do their work.

I use information to make knowledge and if I know something, my judgments may add some credence to you when you use it as information for you to come to the judgments you make as you do your work.

The Role of the Intellectual

From my perspective, this book has been thirty years in the making, long before anyone linked terms such as "knowledge" and "work" and "community" and "practice," or integrated," "digital," and "environment. The book started in 1972 as a part of a series of articles, some of which were published, written in the tradition of the continental thinkers in the 1920's – Gramsci, Korsch and the man who most influenced my intellectual and personal development – Georg Lukacs, with whom I was privileged to work as a young philosopher in Budapest in 1968.

In the post-World War I period, monarchies passed away to be replaced by democracies and socialist regimes of various kinds, new political and social cultures bloomed around the world, and a lively and vibrant intellectual life thrust intellectuals into the very center of political life. One of the major questions of these thinkers, and for all progressives of that era, was the proper function of the intellectual. These thinkers were all intellectuals and the answer to the question of what intellectuals should do was intensely personal as well as theoretical. For me, the problem of the role and function of intellectuals is best understood as a problem of knowledge management.

Forty years later, in the 1960's, many intellectuals were once again thrust into the political world and struggled to answer the question: "What form of organization is appropriate for knowledge and action to be effective?" We were politically active and intellectually curious – two traits which we believed went hand in hand.

Like many other young people of the time, I was involved in both intellectual work and political activity. In 1970 I published a book which summed up the conviction held by many that a new democratic theory was developing in both the East and the West. The new democratic theory would replace the outmoded theories of dialectical materialism and liberal democracies.

Although the political changes did not happen as we thought and hoped, the next forty years brought profound changes that left us with a very different – and new – world in which to live. For the next two decades, after writing the book on political theory, I was involved in very practical political and organizational activities and, later, I developed an increasing fascination with the role and function of information and information technology as an enabler of a new way to do work. In 1983, I walked away from a tumultuous, frustrating and satisfying life as an activist and union president. I had come to know power first hand – how to gather it and how to exercise it. I returned, for a while, to a life of study and contemplation.

I spent nearly a year in the Library of Congress trying to integrate the theory and practice of the transformation of professionals from freestanding thinkers to employees of institutions. I recalled the words of Lukacs during a full day of the two of us walking together in the Hungarian woods. He discussed how even the most abstract thought had practical impact. As he loved to say, "whether or not we solve a particular theoretical problem will not determine whether the revolution will come, but it might make it a little better, a little more humane, when it does come." That advice has motivated my continuing interest in theory – not abstract theory, but theory that comes from and is related to practice.

In 1982, I began writing a book that would be based on empirical studies of what some in the sixties called the "proletarianization" process: the premise of the proposed book would have been that professionals are becoming, not a "new class," but part of productive labor, i.e., part of the working class (the proletariat). The same process of proletarianization and industrialization that Marx described in Capital would, so I thought, apply to these new members of what we, at that time, called "the working class." The same process that peasants went through when they entered the working class applies to intellectuals as they left their freestanding status and became a part of industrial firms as workers.

Tow Truck Operators

In the midst of doing theoretical work, because I needed to make a living, I found myself responding to a request by a group of tow truck operators to help make them into a profession. The practical problem of the tow truck operators was one that I could solve. I thought I knew what a professional does – think for a living. What surprised me was seeing new professions emerging just as the "thinking" professions took on jobs in companies and institutions and became what we now call knowledge workers. The tow truck operators taught me a very important lesson: the proletarianization of the thinker is but one side of the process. Perhaps more important and more interesting is the rise of many new professions – professions of people who are paid to think, paid to take the knowledge of others, use it as information, and formulate new knowledge. As one of the towers explained to me as I watched him teach others how to haul a large truck out of a deep ditch, "It is just physics." Their knowledge takes others' information, processes it through their skills and experience and answers the question: "Is it a good idea to . . . ?" Workers who were once in "menial" jobs are now professionals, a process that we examine in the first chapter.

It was only later that I came to use the term "knowledge worker" to describe the people who are paid to think.

In 1988 I was invited to return to Florida, where I had been organizer and president of a union representing 8,000 faculty and professional employees, to speak at a conference sponsored by the University of Florida – an institution that had fired me (and many others) fifteen years before for our political and social activism. The title of my talk was "Thinking for a Living" – and much of the second chapter of this book is taken from that talk.

Information Technology

By the late 1980's, I had already launched a career in information and began to become familiar with – and fascinated by – the development of information technology. I became a part of the growing field of information management and worked to bring technology to the workplace.

As I worked, I thought often about that unwritten book with the title "Thinking for a Living." In 1999, I fell into one of my most interesting jobs – to create an integrated digital environment for the United States Air Force. Working with members of the military introduced me to many new worlds and to some of the brightest people I have ever met. We came from very different cultures, but we all worked together to try to figure out how to make appropriate use of technology.

This project brought me deeply into both the theory and practice of knowledge work. I was able to bring gifted people together to think and work practically. We concluded that creating an integrated digital environment (one in which we have immediate access to the information we need to do our work) requires a transformation in the work culture.

When that project ended, I returned to the Library of Congress reading room to immerse myself in the literature of knowledge management, change management, and the new "fields" that developed in the last decade. I revisited the topics I considered a generation ago, armed with some new language to help understand a new way to do work.

Transformation

Many people and disciplines observe, discuss and advocate various kinds of transformation. Integration of a number of concepts from various disciplines and practices is the key to work transformation. As the familiar story goes, when a group of blind men touched various parts of the elephant, each described a very different "beast" – one said it was a smooth, pointed animal, another that it was a rough, pliable, thin-skinned one, a third said, no, it was a snake-like beast, long and slim, another opined that it was massive, thick and tough. I hope to provide a sighted-man's view of the elephant.

I am aided in writing this book by a number of important works in anthropology, education, philosophy, business management, psychology, cybernetics, and information technology. It is the integration of these fields that will provide the theory and practice of the new culture that supports knowledge work.

Like knowledge, this book develops spirally. If you read it with your "browser" on, both literally and figuratively, you may dip into the book, then wander off to other "sites" of interest. You might then spiral back and read some more. A book is, by its very nature, serial in character. There is an argument presented here that moves, hopefully, in a logical fashion. I hope it will stimulate your thinking and you will get information from lots of sources, apply your critical thinking facilities, compare it to your experience, contrast it to the accepted norms and turn it into knowledge.

And I hope it contributes to the theory and practice of the growing field of knowledge management.

SECTION I

Work Transforming

In which we examine the changing nature of work in the Knowledge Age.

Our work is, by and large, still done on the industrial model. We come to work. A job is prescribed by management. Tasks are divided and spread out. Coordination of tasks is done by management to achieve the job goal.

The industrial way of working is often no longer efficient. Knowledge work requires an integrated digital environment in which collaborative work takes place. We need a new work culture – one in which information sharing replaces information hoarding. This new culture is developing.

Workers are becoming professionals. They are required to understand the nature and purpose of their work, to know and understand customers and what they need. They work more and more in collaborating teams with a need to understand the whole picture of the environment in which they work. Information is viewed strategically by all levels of workers as a resource to be shared – one that grows in value as it is shared.

Professionals become workers instead of freestanding intellectuals. They work in large organizations where collaboration is required and sharing information can be to the competitive advantage of all parties.

The possibility for collaboration and new technology opens up new ways to work. These changes affect the individual professional and the worker as well as society as a whole. The distinction between professional and worker becomes blurred, rendering the distinction meaningless.

The transformation of the work and work processes is only possible if the work and worker's behavior both change and evolve into a new culture. The change in the nature of work and work process and accompanying change in worker attitudes create the transformation in work culture.

Knowledge work requires thinking . . . it is work where thinking is the essential activity.

Thinking is the creative and critical process that goes into making knowledge.

Key Terms. *(See Glossary for more)*

Culture – The common understandings, language and ways of acting and other assumptions shared by a community.

Knowledge – Justified true belief.

Transformation – A change profound enough to cause a change in the physical, mental, or cultural form of the object or institution.

Work – Force times Distance.

CHAPTER I

Workers Become Professionals

Nothing seems more like work than digging a ditch – it is physical and it is hard. Thinking seems to be the last attribute we might look for in getting a good ditch dug.

However, if you dig ditches for a living today, the way you do that work is likely very different from what it was only a few years ago when you were handed a shovel and told to use your strong back. Today, a ditch digger sits high atop an expensive and complicated piece of machinery. The digger sits in the cabin, which may be air-conditioned. There is probably a computer screen in the cabin that shows the exact requirements for the ditch that needs to be dug. The vast machine is manipulated by an array of knobs and buttons – or, perhaps, by touching a screen that sends directions to the computer that tells the machine what to do.

The work of this professional ditch digger is the same as the man and woman who was handed a shovel and told to move dirt and make a long hole. The work is the same, but the tasks, the qualifications, and expectations of the ditch digger running a computerized back-hoe are very different. The professional ditch-digger needs lots of knowledge and his job is to make judgments – to be certain that the machine is functioning properly, that the proposed ditch is appropriate and that there are no unforeseen obstacles in the way.

The job is to be sure that the hole is "properly" dug and that the machines run "correctly" in doing that job. A ditch is still being dug, but now by a knowledgeable and qualified operator – a knowledge worker who is paid to determine if it is a good idea to dig that ditch there.

The knowledgeable ditch digger works collaboratively as part of a team of other knowledgeable people, many of whom he or she may never meet. Some of those knowledgeable folks have developed plans that include the ditch, perhaps as part of a larger project, but the ditch digger is expected to make adjustments to the plan if the situation at the site indicates.

The leader of the project of which the digging of the ditch is a part of the work needs to respect the knowledge of the ditch digger – and expect the ditch digger to use judgment when doing the work.

But in the end, it is up to the ditch digger to make certain that it is good idea to do what needs to be done and that the computer and the machine properly does what he has decided that they should do. In order to do the work of ditch digging today, the worker needs to understand lots of things. He or she needs to be a knowledge worker.

From Menials to Professionals

The transformation of what we once called "menial" labor into professional labor – is driven by a realization that work is done better and faster if there is involvement of those who do the work. Although workers have always been involved in the work that they do, knowledge work requires a higher degree of commitment, understanding, and responsibility for work. Collaborative work is proving to be a much more efficient way to organize industrial production than the assembly line. Knowledgeable workers are an asset throughout an organization. The transformation of menial labor into professional labor – knowledge work – is made possible through automation. Automation, itself, does turn menial labor into knowledge work, but it does eliminate one kind of work that can better be done by a machine and replace it with another work which requires knowledge and understanding.

Quality Circles and Quality Improvement began the process of professionalizing the work force. These business practices, like many of those that go to make up the new work culture, were initiated in Japan.

The Japanese, after being decimated in war, put the values of their culture to work to build and develop a modern industrialized society. They did this by focusing on involving the work force in every aspect of production. The Japanese were faced with a major crisis in their society – losing a war that decimated their industrial society. The transformation of the way they worked was not, initially at least, motivated by their desire for change, but by significant emotional and physical events beyond their control.

They became an industrial power by emphasizing quality – where quality is defined as what meets the needs of customers. Quality improvement was codified in a very specific methodology and became a means to make dramatic changes in the way work is done.

A related, but different, movement developed around reengineering – a methodology designed and developed to create new business processes. Reengineering is one of the tools used to bring about and manage change and is now part and parcel of the thinking and attitudes of management.

The emphasis on reengineering and meeting customer needs by providing quality products both rely on developing new ways to do work that bring people into collaborative relationships.

The transformation of menial work into knowledge work is perhaps seen most clearly in the service industry and manufacturing. But similar processes are under way in a large number of fields that bring attitudes and ways of working that were once the sole purview of professionals to whole new groups of workers.

The Airplane Mechanic

Today's mechanic, like today's ditch digger, is a knowledge worker. The work has been transformed into professional work where knowledge and thinking replaces the brute force that once characterized most work. The output of the mechanic, like that of the ditch digger is a judgment – that the airplane is working properly and can be flown. It is up to the mechanic to determine if the airplane is trustworthy and safe.[5]

The mechanic is the center of the work of making sure that a plane is flight-worthy. The testing and evaluation of the plane takes place while it is in flight and the results are sent ahead so that the necessary work can be scheduled, parts ordered, etc. Information about the history of the plane, what work has been done, what regular maintenance is due, and what modifications need to be made are collected together in an integrated data system. All of the necessary parts are ordered and available before the plane comes into the hanger.

---

[5] The author is indebted to the wonderful mechanics at Robins Air Force Base and to Anthony Adamson, who worked to dramatically improve the quality of their work – and their work life – through business re-engineering.

The mechanic is like the skilled surgeon in an operating room. Physical activity takes place – but what counts is that the mechanic is knowl edgeable and can make the judgments necessary to answer the question: "Is this plane ready to fly?"

And – along the way, the mechanic is expected to notice similarities and anomalies and raise questions that may, using computers to access a myriad of databases, answers questions that lead to modifications to correct problems for a whole class of airplanes.

It is the knowledge of the mechanic and properly applying that knowledge while collaborating with a team of people, few of whom he or she may meet in person, that makes this mechanic a knowledge worker.

Retail/Service Industry

The retail business has been the subject of considerable interest by knowledge management theorists. Perhaps the most interesting is Ikujiro Nonaka, the Japanese business theorist, who focuses on knowledge creation and its use in businesses. He describes the transformation in two businesses, Seven-Eleven Japan and Wal-Mart, with very different cultures and ways of doing business, but both "strive to achieve similar results – to create knowledge."[6]

In 1973, Ito-Yakado, a Japanese Supermarket Chain and Southland Corporation, the owner of Seven-Eleven convenience stores in the United States, entered into a licensing agreement. The first stores were opened in Japan in 1978 and in 1991 Ito-Yakado acquired Seven-Eleven. Nonaka describes their business as follows:

> *"Seven-Eleven Japan . . . is a franchiser that sells knowledge. The company charges its franchisees for services, receives royalties for trademarks, and collects leasing fees for equipment such as information systems, display racks, and refrigerated cases. To provide these services to the franchisees, Seven-Eleven Japan makes extensive use of quintessential explicit knowledge . . .[7]*

---

[6] "Two Case Studies, Seven-Eleven Japan and Wal-Mart" in "Integrated Information Technology Systems for Knowledge Creation" by Ikujiro Nonaka, Patrick Reinmoller, and Ryoko Toyama in Handbook of Organizational Learning and Knowledge." Oxford: Oxford University Press, p. 835.
[7] Ibid., p. 837.

"The key to understanding Seven-Eleven Japan is its successful use of IT (information technology) together with human-based systems. ... Store owners and part-time employees alike can place orders ... They gain tacit knowledge through experience-based institutions ... Human insight, not IT, makes the difference."[8]

The process that Nonaka describes is one that we will, later in the book, call "spiral thinking" or "abductive reasoning." He describes that process as follows:

"Selected hypothesis are presented at headquarters during a weekly conference attended by all field counselors, top management, and headquarters staff .... Seven-Eleven Japan emphasizes the importance of context for knowledge creation . . . .

"Seven-Eleven triggers action and reflection in four phases:

(a) IT (information technology) is used as a trigger for the conversion of frontline knowledge into ideas.

(b) Insights of employees trigger experimentation with the POS (point of sale) data

(c) Verification of hypotheses in the database leads to experimentation in other regions.

(d) Justified new knowledge (proven hypotheses) is disseminated among and utilized in all stores ...

Thus Seven-Eleven uses a series of triggers that alternate between action and reflection."[9]

As we shall see later, the combination of action and reflection is at the core of knowledge work. What happens at a particular store, in a particular community, is particular to that store. The insights of the employees at the various stores need to be gathered together and synthesized in order to meet the needs of the organization as a whole. Once this new knowledge is adopted, it is then made available to all of the stores. This process depends upon a high level of automation in the work place so that information is accessible throughout the enterprise.

It also depends on developing a new work culture and way of doing work. The process of knowledge work involves developing hypotheses,

---

[8] Ibid., p. 838.
[9] Ibid., p. 840.

testing them, and disseminating the knowledge gained throughout the business. This process, and the understanding that comes with it, is known as abduction and is characteristic of knowledge work.

A similar discussion of Wal-Mart leads to the same conclusion, but from the point of view of large retail outlets selling large quantities at the lowest possible cost. Seven-Eleven sells relatively small quantities to repeat customers with a high profit margin. Both see the task of retailing to be knowledge management.

What makes Seven-Eleven and Wal-Mart successful throughout the world is that they are able to deliver specific goods and services to very specific clientele and neighborhoods efficiently.

Nonaka describes the environment in which the customer/client and their particular needs are quickly identified by the associates at the store level and made available to everyone throughout the company. For example, if there were a basketball tournament in a small city in Indiana, local associates know that information. The local community in Indiana understands the importance of basketball and can make certain that their stores have ample supplies of beer, colas, chips, etc. on hand for this important event. It is important in just one community, but knowing communities is what retailing is about – and this work must be done one community at a time.

Technology enables information from communities throughout an enterprise to be gathered, analyzed and made available to be turned into knowledge. Stocking is done on a daily basis. Knowledge gathered by staff at the various stores is a valuable commodity and workers are empowered to order what is needed, based on their knowledge of the community in which they work.

All of this knowledge is gathered together, analyzed and used as the basis for managing the company. By relying on those closest to the customers to make basic business decisions, within the context of a large company that delivers consistent quality and reasonable service, a whole new concept of neighborhood stores was born.

Wal-Mart, which grew out of a single store in Arkansas, adopted many of the same basic principles. Wal-Mart focused on eliminating intermediaries wherever possible. Direct lines from the manufacturer to the consumer replace the wholesalers, with Wal-Mart serving as the organizer of the service. Products remain the property of the manufacturer and manufacturers are linked directly to the point of sales systems so that deliveries are made to replenish inventories without extensive human intervention. Making sales information accessible to manufacturers enables them to do their work more effectively with savings to the company.

Sales clerks are associates and stockholders. The Wal-Mart Foundation, which is widely advertised and promoted in the store, supports community-based organizations. The focus is on serving at the community level . . . on the particular needs of a particular set of people.

The Wal-Mart story is not a simple or uncontroversial one. Many communities saw their landscape transformed by the arrival of the Big Box and some won battles against the large corporation that they saw coming to destroy their community. Many critics and some employees question employment practices that appear to be discriminatory. The point in this discussion is not to portray Wal-Mart as the perfect company, but show how work is being transformed in all parts of society. As one observer put it, "Piece by piece, Wal-Mart was building a system that would give its executives a complete picture, at any point in time, of where goods were and how fast they were moving, all the way from the factory to the checkout counter."[10]

Traditional retailers focused on how best to sell the same merchandise as widely as possible. They saw retailing from the viewpoint of the goods they want to sell. Wal-Mart and Seven-Eleven, on the other hand, see retailing from the viewpoint of the customer, not what is being sold. Before Wal-Mart and Seven-Eleven goods were manufactured in large plants, sent to wholesalers who stored them and through a sales and delivery network, transferred the goods to retailers who sold them to the public. The job was to convince people to buy what the factories made. Both Wal-Mart and Seven-Eleven Japan (and many other companies that imitate them) looked at the process from a very different point of view. Retailing is a form of knowledge management. Instead of gathering all resources into headquarters, a deliberate effort is made to spread the resources throughout the enterprise. Knowledge of what is going on in the community-based stores is the most valuable commodity of the enterprise.

At least in theory, workers are valued for the knowledge that they have . . . what they know about the products, what the products can do . . . and most importantly the community in which the store lives, i.e. their work, takes on many of the traditional characteristic of professionals.

Wal-Mart takes the importance of marketing to a community beyond the distribution of goods. The "good works" of the Wal-Mart foundation becomes an important part of the business. Employees are encouraged to "volunteer" their services to the community. Wal-Mart advertising focuses as much on the social life found in the store as it does on the low cost of the goods that are for sale.

---

[10] Ortega, Bob, In Sam We Trust. The Untold Story of Sam Walton and how Wal-Mart is Devouring American. Random House, 1998, p. 130.

Doing good works and selling to communities is not confined to Wal-Mart. A flyer in the local Starbucks Coffee house, promotes the Starbuck Foundation ("Hope, Discovery and Opportunity in Starbucks Communities"), which is a reflection of the company's commitment to support our communities and embrace diversity. The Foundation receives funding from Starbucks Coffee Company and from individual donations."

Wal-Mart employees are called "associates," the same term used in law firms, and they are expected to participate enthusiastically in community life. Their work follows them home – and the company expects their work to go beyond putting in time at the store.

Both Wal-Mart and 7–11 create a direct link between suppliers of products and customers. This link is possible only if information easily and regularly turns into knowledge. Employees are paid to think and their judgments about what needs to be done are not only welcomed, but acted upon. Knowledge is community-based. Decisions are related to those who know the community and its needs.

The linkage of suppliers to customers gives a whole new meaning to retail . . . for it is retail without wholesale.

Forms Management and Data Capture

A form is a way to collect information in a uniform manner so that it can be captured and used. Data capture using various forms of recognition – bar codes, marks on paper, and optical character recognition – are now a normal part of our lives. A form is a way to control and capture data and information . . . to make it fit into a pre-conceived scheme. A paper form is a database on paper. A database is a paper form put into the electronic world.

An entire industry has grown up to manage these forms. Document management – the management of thousand and hundreds of thousands of forms is one of the most highly automated sectors in our information society.[11]

Huge industries exist to manage forms. Forms management is particularly important for banks (check processing), insurance companies (claim processing), mass marketing companies (fulfilling requests), and government (census, tax collection, and law enforcement and criminal justice).

The act of "automating" forms, like most automation, began as a process of doing the same work processes with machines that had previously been done with paper.

---

[11] See Megill, Kenneth A. and Schantz, Herb. Document Management.

The emphasis of this automation focuses on data capture and uses technologies such as optical character recognition (sometimes called intelligent character recognition) that enables a machine to read and enables the processing of paper forms to be automated.

The forms processing industry has now gone far beyond capturing data and focuses on work process improvement.

When Etienne Wenger describes a "community of practice," he chooses the work of insurance claims processing. He describes in considerable detail how this work, which appears to be routine, is actually done within a context of a community of practice. What appears to be the most routine, boring assembly line, upon examination by an anthropoligist/sociologist/cybernetician, becomes a rich and varied set of activities . . . many social in nature.

Etienne Wenger describes the world of the claims examiner as follows:

"Although claims processors may appear to work individually, and though their jobs are primarily defined and organized individually, processes become important to each other. When I asked what they thought they would remember about this job later in life, the response was almost always, "the people." They are quite aware of their interdependence in making the job possible and the atmosphere pleasant. They act as resources to each other, exchanging information, making sense of situations, sharing new tricks and new ideas, as well as keeping each other company and spicing up each other's working days."[12]

Effectiveness in claims processing comes by improving workflows . . . by eliminating the number of steps in the chain that the claim travels through.

Accuracy comes from what is called "data purification" – using look-up databases and information about the community from which the forms emerge – to improve the accuracy of the work.

Claims processing uses many of the same technologies that are applied in other industries where data needs to read and captured. For example, the post office sorts mail using optical recognition of addresses that are printed or written on a large variety of envelopes with a plethora of handwriting styles. The recognition of the addresses is accurately done by machines because the information systems managing the data capture can

---

[12] Etienne Wenger, Community of Practice. Cambridge: Cambridge University Press, 1998). p. 47–48. We will discuss the concept of community of practice later.

compare what it "thinks" the character may be with databases that contain zip codes, names of cities and towns, and street names. Insurance companies processing health claim forms have extensive databases composed of names of doctors, hospitals, diagnoses, and drugs. While processing the claim form, quality control and fraud detection is built into the process of form recognition.

Efficiencies come, therefore, not just by speeding up the process of reading and processing forms (improving the workflow), but also from improved work processes. Machines, especially computers, replace large offices organized on an assembly-line leaving the "real" work – the knowledge work of making judgments as to what the correct address is when the machine is in doubt, whether a claim should be processed, and so forth to the knowledge worker. The machine cannot do some tasks as accurately as a human being who applies judgments but it can do routine tasks much faster. Even the lowest worker in the chain becomes a knowledge worker who needs to understand and know the nature and purpose of the work of the organization in order to be most efficient. As the automation process proceeds, forms are eliminated and replaced by managing the knowledge of a community.

Judgments can, to a certain extent, be automated when they are routine and similar, but these judgments all take place within a community of practice, with its own way of doing work, its own language, and its own way of accomplishing its work.

Forms management is now a matter of quality control, sharing information used by a community across individual and company lines, and making information immediately accessible to those who need it to do their business.

But forms management today shows that what appears to be the most bureaucratic and routine functions of all turn out, when properly organized, to be knowledge work in an information-sharing environment that is highly social in nature. The social interaction of workers in a community and their empowerment to make appropriate decisions is necessary as the forms management processes are automated and a new culture of work emerges.

Manufacturing: From Assembly Line to Quality Circles

The auto industry was the paradigm of the modern industrial mode of production. Henry Ford introduced a radical concept for work – the assembly line, touted as the "scientific" way to do work.

A complex task, making the automobile, was broken into thousands of discrete tasks and laid out along an assembly line. Workers remained stationary while cars moved from one end of the line to the other. Production was controlled and regulated by the line. Efficiencies came as workers were able to do a discrete task faster and faster. As they improved, the line was sped up.

Workers were organized as an industrial army with hierarchical command structures. Levels of supervision were imposed to keep the line running and to devise new ways to speed up the line.

Time and motion studies rationalized each task as it was made increasingly routine. The rationalization process is at the heart of applying "scientific" principles to industrial processes. In this sense, science is understood as a process of observing and simplifying so that redundant tasks can be eliminated and the assembly line sped up. The assembly line form of work proved to be incredibly productive and was widely applied far beyond the production of large and complex machines like the automobile.

As time went on, however, the straight-line form of production gave way to a newer, more efficient, process based on collaboration. The transformation of automobile production to a team-driven activity had many causes. One cause was that the work force sabotaged the line – slowed it down, making it more humane and more interesting. Then workers organized into industrial unions to be a counter-point to industrial management and the trade union was transformed from a guild organized around a particular skill or capability, to an army of its own. Industrial warfare followed.

An accord was reached and relative peace brought to the work place as trade unions and management agreed on how to keep the machines and the line running efficiently and effectively. In several instances, particularly in Europe, representatives of the trade unions joined the board of directors. However, the struggle for control continued.

The introduction of computers and information-driven processes to the work place in the second half of the twentieth century brought another revolution. Tools are now available to take over a host of tasks that previously required human intervention. Other tools offer opportunities for collaboration to take place throughout the work process. Information, learning and sharing become the reigning values.

When the twenty-first century dawned, the assembly line was still the norm for industrial production, but new values gained dominance, often led by the auto industry, that require new ways to do work. Instead of breaking down tasks, they are integrated. Instead of each person doing only one task at a time, it is shown that, from the viewpoint of the product and customer satisfaction, the most productive way to do work is through collaboration. Collaborative work entered manufacturing. This transformation to collaboration in the work place establishes a premium value on information sharing.

The demise of the traditional assembly line mode of production began in Japan, but was quickly transferred to the industrial heartland, the United States and Europe. Like all transformation of work, the move away from assembly line to collaborative work takes place over time, but spreads world-wide as international companies seek the best and most efficient places to make their products.

Seniority and life-long jobs become less and less the hallmark of a good worker. Whole industries simply get up and move to a new place or a new country to get the kind of less expensive and more flexible work force needed for maximum efficiency.

However, the "industrial" worker is being transformed into a knowledge worker, who is responsible for understanding the nature of the work and the purpose for which it is done. The knowledge worker involves and invokes judgment in all aspects of work. The knowledge worker works collaboratively and, in the end, collaborative work becomes more efficient than even the cheapest labor in the industrial model that relies on reducing all work to simple tasks. Factories which move to countries, where cheap labor is the only commodity discover that they need, in order to produce quality products, an environment in which knowledge workers are available. Sometimes this process simply pushes industries on to an even cheaper place for manufacturing. For example, Singapore began as a manufacturing center, but within twenty-five years after its independence it had become a center for knowledge work and knowledge workers.

Education – From the Box to the Team

A teacher in a box is still the model for many people – except for teachers who understand that a new way to do the work of education is needed. In the box, the teacher stands in front of the room and controls the environment while dispensing knowledge, the amount of knowledge successfully dispensed is measured by standardized tests.

Although the model pervades our assumptions about what education and learning are all about, the reality is moving rapidly in another direction. Learning is replacing training. Understanding is becoming more important than adding new skills. Making knowledge, by assimilating and understanding information, is becoming the norm. The good teachers know they need to teach judgment-making, evaluation and creativity.

However, education is still very much a matter of accumulating credits – discrete units that, added together, bring a degree. But certification that measures competencies, whether granted by professional associations or businesses, is replacing degrees as the sign of the most effective and efficient worker. Testing for competencies, rather than attendance and participation in formal educational programs, focuses on a knowledge base and how well a particular person masters that base. The purpose of competency-based certification is to determine whether someone is competent to do a particular kind of work, not whether they sat through a prescribed program.

The world of education is being blown apart as technology moves beyond the assembly line to learning. Collaboration is a more efficient way to do work – and gets better results, whether this work is done in a factory or in a school. Teams of people can deliver more learning faster and better than a lone teacher.

Technology makes it possible a student to "sit" in a virtual classroom with others who may be in many different parts of the country or the world. At the same time, standardized tests become nation-wide and worldwide and teaching is a matter of meeting norms, leaving no student behind and delivering uniform products. The key drives to bring technology and standardization to the classroom is ubiquitous.

The "standardization" of teaching flies in the face, however, of much of what we know about learning – how we learn in context, in community. Being an apprentice who learns "peripherally"[13] is the kind of learning most appropriate in knowledge situations.

Teachers, like other traditional professionals – doctors, lawyers, priests – become responsible for the direction and management of para-professionals and other "support" personal, who, in turn, take on more and more of the work once done by professionals.

The rapid rise of knowledge work demands a new kind of product from educational institutions – a creative thinker or a computer literate person who can also write. The knowledge worker needs to be able to play games and improvise, see connections, and work with a team-oriented customer-driven set of values.

---

[13] See Lave, Jean and Etienne Wenger, Situated Learning. Legitimate Peripheral Participation. Cambridge: Cambridge University Press, 1991.

Education returns to communities. Charter schools flourish by meeting particular needs for particular groups of people – all within a new set of emerging values: sharing, collaboration, quality control and flexibility.

Thinking for a living demands new kinds of learning for thinkers: those who know how to integrate, make choices, innovate and synthesize – the skills of the knowledge worker.

Military – Network Centric Warfare

The notion of community-based, rather than hierarchical relationship finds its way into every phase of our work life – even those that we may think must necessarily be hierarchical in character, like the military. The new military professionals must collaborate closely with the communities of which they are a part. The knowledge created in these communities is critical to the military professionals' survival.

The military is nearly everyone's idea of the best example a top-down, hierarchical organization – the very model of an industrial enterprise. "Modern" warfare developed on the industrial model – armies moving across terrain to capture and control land. War became a matter of logistics – getting the people and material to the right place at the right time.

Actually, an effective military relies more on leadership than obeying orders – particularly as the electronic world comes to dominate war, just as it does every other phase of life. Leadership is one of the most important attributes of a knowledge worker – and the military has long experience in creating leaders. The ability to present one's justified beliefs – knowledge – in a way that others in the community can adopt them is important for everyone involved in knowledge enterprises.

Non-hierarchical does not mean disorderly or being incapable of making a decision. Indeed, communities of practices, through their leaders, make decisions that guide and infuse the entire community.

A new doctrine of warfare, with many names, is emerging for the knowledge age. The new concept of warfare sometimes goes under the name of "network centric warfare."

This doctrine brings with it a new work culture, new requirements for the military "worker" and a professionalization of war. The winner of industrial wars was often the country that could mobilize the largest number of people in the fastest time to go to the "front" and defeat the other army. Conscription, involuntary labor, is the norm in the industrialized army.

The new, professional, military requires a very different kind of work ethic. It requires a trained, educated and thinking soldier, sailor or airman who is motivated to do more than follow orders. Perhaps this transformation is best captured by the latest recruiting slogan adopted by the US Army – "An Army of One." This slogan replaced "Be the Best You Can Be."

Like all slogans, this one carries various, sometimes contradictory, meanings with it. At first glance, it might mean that the spirit of cooperation in the previous slogan is replaced by a kind of naked individualism in which a person is no longer dependent on other workers for success. However, the slogan also implies that you are not necessarily the best operating under someone else's orders. The new slogan implies an independent person. The next step, to flesh out the slogan and describe the proper role of the war fighter to be "an army of one," working within a community.

"War is a product of its age. The tools and tactics of how we fight have always evolved along with technology . . . . Warfare in the Information Age will inevitably embody the characteristics that distinguish this age from previous ones."[14]

The term "network centric warfare" is contrasted with "platform-centric warfare" and is defined in convoluted language appropriate to texts emerging out of the Department of Defense as

"an information superiority-enabled concept of operations that generates increased combat power by networking sensors, decision makers, and shooters to achieve shared awareness, increased speed of command, higher tempo of operations, greater lethality, increased survivability, and a degree of self-synchronization."[15]

Words like "shooters" emphasize that real warfare is being talked about here . . . warfare that takes on a very different character than armies

---

[14] Alberts, David S., John J. Garstka and Frederick P. Stein. Network Centric Warfare: Developing and Leveraging Information Superiority. Washington DC: National Defense University Press, 1999. p. 15. Also available from in digital form from The Command and Control Research Program (CCRP) within the United States Department of Defense. http://www.dodccrp.org/
[15] Ibid, p. 16

moving across territory. It requires, in their words, "a degree of self-synchronization" the ability for those doing the work to think.

Network centric warfare "translates information superiority into combat power by effectively linking knowledgeable entities in the battle-space."[16]

The book goes into considerable detail about the emerging nature of warfare. It emphasizes that network centric warfare

> *"is not about turning the battle over to 'the network' or even relying more on automated tools and decision aids. It is really about exploiting information to maximize combat power by bringing more of our available information and warfighting assets to bear both effectively and efficiently. NCW (network centric warfare) is about developing collaborative working environments . . . to make it easier to develop common perceptions of the situation and achieve (self-) coordinated responses to situations."[17]*

The important point, from our perspective, is the insertion of "(self-)" into the text, which makes all of the difference in the nature of work. An army of one is needed. Soldiers need to be self-coordinated knowledge workers working collectively within a community.

A network centric environment is very different from a centralized command environment. It operates by linking communities . . . in principle an infinite number of communities can be linked through networks, while each community retains its identity.

Work goes on in the individual nodes or communities that are linked together. Different people do very different work and the web that develops to link together this work is very different from the control model.

The practical implications for how wars are fought are still being worked out and go beyond our discussion here. What is interesting and noteworthy is that even in the heart of the most hierarchal organizational structures in our society, an understanding of the importance of knowledge and the work done by knowledge workers is present.

The military recognizes that centralized command is still necessary for the military (as it is for any kind of large and complex organization). However, "control" needs to be understood more in terms of leadership

---

[16] Ibid., p. 26.
[17] Ibid., p. 26.

than management and direction. Leadership involves bringing people along and motivating them to take on common tasks. No kind of organization has more experience in leadership than the military. The concept of network centric warfare recognizes that centralized direction may no longer be the most efficient way to get work done – at least as it is traditionally understood. The network centric environment is a way to describe this new way to do work. It is a profound shift in understanding the relationships among those who lead and those who follow. It is another example of the professionalization of work and the importance of thinking for a living.

Medicine – the End of the Super Doctor

Peter Drucker identifies the modern hospital as one of the three paradigms for knowledge work (the symphony orchestra and the university are the other two).[18]

Drucker looks at the modern hospital as a small group of people (the doctors) controlling a large army of workers.

The work in medical facilities is increasingly carried on by teams of professionals and para-professionals with more and more work being done by technicians. The traditional professions, the nurses, doctors, and social workers are transformed into managers and directors of teams of technicians.

These technicians require an increasing understanding of the work that they do and the ability to function as knowledge workers. The professionals (as we shall see in the next chapter) undergo a transformation into "workers" just as the "workers" take on more and more of the traditional work of the professional – the knowledge work.

A closer look shows something very different happening – the emergence of teams, cooperation and even collaboration as the characteristics of the efficient and effective practice of medicine.

As the cost of industrial-style medical care skyrockets – and its success creates an older and older patient population – new kinds of medicine emerge based on holistic and environmental ways of looking at the patient.

Health management, rather than "curing" sick people, focuses on preserving health and preventing illness. New kinds of practitioners are

---

[18] Peter Drucker, "The Coming New Organization." The Harvard Business Review on Knowledge Management. Boston: Harvard Business School Press, 1998. We shall look more closely at Drucker's view later.

accepted as part of a team that focuses on improving the quality of life through exercise, good nutrition and satisfying human activities. Even death itself is seen less as an indication of failure by the medical system and more as a natural event in life.

The modern industrial hospital, with the super doctor at the top of the heap turns out to be just as inefficient as the assembly lines in manufacturing. Computers replace guessing in the medical world.

Cooperation, collaboration, and information sharing are values of the new health care professionals who work together as a team to focus on the patient in a community.

You don't need to transport patients to a central repository – the hospital – in order to have access to the knowledge needed for good health. This knowledge can be delivered anywhere, any time to patients within a community.

Many More

We could give many more examples of jobs that were once seen to be routine or industrial becoming knowledge jobs – where the primary product is knowledge that becomes information for others to use.

These examples are, we think, enough to make the point that all work is in the process of being transformed into knowledge work. The transition is not complete, but it is underway.

Even in the so-called developing world, an increasing portion of the population is engaged in what is now called knowledge work. In fact, we can sometimes see instances where historical epochs are skipped. Technologies that underlie the knowledge age are being rapidly transferred and adopted by societies at all levels of development.

The knowledge age is still coming – and is not yet here, but we can see it developing and new ways of work emerging. The paradigms are changing . . . sometimes subtly and gradually and sometimes suddenly.

From ditch-diggers to military troops – from sales clerks to teachers – knowledge work is becoming the expected norm. The process of professionals becoming workers and workers becoming professionals is widespread and seems to be moving rapidly throughout the world. What we once called professionals can now best be described as knowledge workers. We turn our attention to them.

CHAPTER 2

Professionals Become Workers

Thinking, when it is done for a living, has value to someone else – an employer, or a community. Not all thinking is associated with work, but when it is, the value of the work is determined by someone other than the creator.

Thinking is a social act. It takes place within a context, within a history, and within a culture. Thinking is, some say, what differentiates us from the other creatures on this earth. When thinking is done for someone else and is recognized and paid for, then it becomes knowledge work – thinking for a living. Not all thinking, of course, is work and not all work is thinking work. But when we think for a living, we do knowledge work.

There is no such thing as pure thought. Thought is always done in a context, out of a situation with a history and culture. Thinking is transformational in nature. Thought is closely linked to practice.

And thinking is critical. It is an activity that calls into question. As Socrates put it, thinking is examining "those who think that they are wise when they are not – an experience which has its amusing side." And we all, from time to time, think we are wise and then another thinker comes along and examines what we claim to know . . . and calls into doubt beliefs that we thought were true and justified.

Thinking can rarely be simplified . . . although it can be elegant. The essence of thinking is complicating, comparing, questioning, searching – and then distilling, discarding, focusing, and coming to a judgment . . . "Is it a good idea to . . . ?" This question – and answering of this question – is at the heart of knowledge work.

We will talk a lot about knowledge work . . . what it is and what we do when we "make" knowledge. Making knowledge requires thinking . . . lots of it. Thinking is an activity that can be surprising and gratifying and, sometimes, it even makes our heads hurt.

Making Thinking into Work and Work into Thinking Work

Work is, when it is thinking work, playful in nature. As thinking becomes work it must retain its voluntary character – and even be fun – if it is to be done well. As Tom Sawyer said, "Play consists of whatever a body is not obliged to do." You cannot oblige people to think.

You can encourage them to think. You can give incentives and create good work environments. You can make sure that they have the right tools and access to the information they need to do their work. You can lead. But, in the end, you cannot oblige someone to think. They have to want to do it – and good thinking, like good play, is a pleasurable experience.

For most of history, man has worked to meet his needs with an environment where thought plays little role in the productive process. Tradition/experience, or frozen thought, dictates how work is done. Knowledge is the conclusion of a community – a result of critical thinking. If you do work as it has "always" been done – as tradition tells you to do it, it is not necessary for the worker to think. In fact, to challenge the way things are done can be a subversive act. The person or persons doing work did so to meet his needs and create useful things that could be traded for things made by others. Work resulted in immediately useful products that could be used, stored or exchanged.

With the introduction of manufacturing, labor came under a new kind of discipline – a discipline dictated by the machine. The discipline of the machine is thoughtless. It is a force external to the work process. As work moved from manufacturing to an industrial mode of production, the machine took over the production of goods – and the worker became an appendage to the machine. The worker sold time to "operate" the machine and the products belonged to the owner of the machines.

The process of the alienation of work, a necessary process for work to become a job, is based on exchange – making labor-time a product like any other product so that labor time can be bought and sold. The control of the work time, once it is sold, passes to the owner of the time, the employer.

Once labor time becomes a commodity – when it is bought and sold – it becomes alienated – it loses its human function.

Intellectual work, like other work, has a use value. The intellectual provides assistance, or solace, in a time of need and is paid in goods that sustain the intellectual. The history of the industrialization of intellectual labor corresponds with that of other work, with the same consequences: alienation, separation from community, and loss of control of work time.

As professionals become part of the work process, many of the tasks once performed by professionals are transferred to technicians, often working under the direction of professionals. A further separation from the work takes place as the professional begins to assume managerial functions.

The number of technicians necessary for productive labor increases rapidly. Teachers, doctors, nurses and laboratory scientists become the minority as they are increasingly dependent on technicians and aides to get the work done. The thinker is caught in the firing line between the directors, who have control of the needed resources, and the technicians who do the work.

Once the work is simplified and divided, it becomes possible to contract out much of the work. Sometimes the subcontracting takes on the form of delegating whole tasks to specialists in another location. Other times, it comes by hiring part-time and temporary workers to perform tasks.

Once the cost of machinery becomes the primary cost of operations (rather than the cost of personnel), as it does in scientific laboratories, medicine and the military, to name a few, decisions are made on the basis of what will increase the efficiency of the machines.

The term traditionally used for those who make their living by thinking is "intellectual." This term is much more prevalent in Europe than it is in the United States, which has not had a class of intellectuals. The life of the intellectual was not idyllic even before professional work became industrialized. In fact, intellectuals and professionals often lived on the fringe of society and were often barely tolerated. They were not seen as a productive part of society. Once they entered into the industrialized work world, their work became valued and valuable, but the independence that was a hallmark of their earlier life disappeared.[19]

---

[19] When I began to study philosophy in the university, I was fascinated at how philosophers made a living. Most "modern" philosophers (the term for Western philosophy from Descartes to Hegel) were attached to royal courts – along with musicians, jesters and artists.

The Life of the Intellectual

The French philosopher Descartes had a particularly rotten life. He had his great idea ("I think therefore, I am") while he was inside an oven – no doubt trying to escape the frigid cold of Northern Europe. He died an ignoble death after catching a cold because he had to get up early to tutor the offspring of a Scandinavian noble family – the cold floors were just too much for him.

Socrates had it even harder. He enjoyed a good life (as evidence in the good party described in the Symposium). He did not have to worry about cold floors, for he lived in sunny Greece. But he did have to worry about the public-spirited citizens of his day who were troubled because he was corrupting their youth.

Like many a good teacher, Socrates was rather proud of the fact that the youth who crossed his path were transformed. He understood that the search for knowledge is a matter of learning how to ask the right questions.

Yet Socrates was tried and found guilty of corrupting the youth. He was executed by the State. At his trial, Socrates proposed an interesting punishment for his crime: "Well, what is appropriate for a poor man who is a public benefactor and who requires leisure for giving you moral encouragement? Nothing could be more appropriate for such a person than free maintenance at the state's expense." (Apology, 36(d))

Those in charge of his trial did not take kindly to his suggestion, so in the end he drank the hemlock. Some of his students tried to talk him out of taking the poison. They arranged for him to escape and go abroad, but he rejected their arguments. He knew that he should be paid to think – that was his job – and if the penalty was to drink the hemlock, so be it.

Since Socrates, many thinkers have come and gone and more than one has been subjected to ridicule and punishment for calling into question the accepted and understood knowledge of the day. But thinking is still a prized activity and a lucky few, often called professionals, have been fortunate to be paid to think. Now more and more people are paid to think. And professionals are often organized in the work place and in society.

The professionalization we discussed in the previous chapter of what was thought of as "menial" labor is just one side of the coin. Professionals, people who were once thought to be apart from the industrial world, are becoming socialized into the broader society and their work more mechanized. Their work is characterized by a high degree of cooperation found in the industrial world, which leads to a new kind of professional collaboration.

As professionals become part of the industrialized work force and the industrialized work force takes on the characteristics of professionals, collaboration becomes the norm. But what professionals do and what they think of themselves is often very different. When the market place enters, the vocation or calling is transformed into a job. As they become part of the industrial work force, a sharp distinction is drawn between their work time and free time. The special status traditionally given to professionals disappears as they begin to punch the clock.

Thinking as a job becomes routine, in the sense that it is not just the purview of the privileged, but is a universal character of work. This loss of status is sometimes uncomfortable for the professional worker, who often was paid in terms of prestige rather than money[20]. The "specialness" of professional work – thinking for a living – is disappearing.

Except for the fortunate few who enter this world with wealth and position endowed to them, we work for a living. Professionals are those paid to think as their work. We all think – what makes the professional different is the context in which the thought goes on – whether or not we are paid to think.

The professional sells his thought as a commodity that is consumed, transformed and passed on. Economists now speak of "intellectual capital" and are working to find ways to measure and account for intellectual assets.

Although working for a living is not universally admired, thinking is. When thinking becomes a way of making a living, tensions arise. In fact, according to the American myth, the sons and daughters of the poor work their way into the middle class and go to college so they can become doctors or teachers so they don't have to work – at least not in the way their parents did. But anyone who has a professional job today knows that thinking is a way of working. Being part of a working class is an honorable way to spend one's life – even if that work is professional in nature.

Workers create products for a living, things that can be bought and sold. When professionals become workers, the commodity (product) they sell is their thinking, their decision-making power, their ability to take information and turn it into knowledge. Once the professional enters into the industrialized setting, then thinking is sold as labor time. Stresses and

---

[20] The liberal arts, the gateway to the professions, were once seen as the domain of the gentleman. The Oxford English Dictionary says this in its number 1 definition of liberal: "Originally the distinctive epithet of those 'arts' or 'sciences' that were considered 'worthy of the free man' opposed to servile or mechanical."

strains emerge, because decision-making and knowledge creation are not activities that can be easily scheduled and coordinated.

Becoming a worker brings with it a new relationship to the products of the professional's labor. These are now owned by the company for which they work. The company and the company's policies determine the relationship of the worker to the customer or client. The professional no longer deals directly with the client. This process separates the professional from the knowledge products and alienates the knowledge worker. The work of the professional in an industrial setting is brought under discipline and control – is managed and planned – just as manual labor is brought under control in the manufacturing process. Just as the industrial age took tasks that were done in manufacturing, rationalized them and turned them into activities that are driven by and controlled by the machine, so technology is now becoming a normal and accepted part of thinking work. No longer can a knowledge worker afford to be anti-technological.

The computer's capabilities drive and control intellectual work in an industrial setting. In the knowledge age, this force is turned around as thinking collaboratively becomes widespread and technologies emerge that enable collaborative work to become the norm.

Thinking for a living is becoming a mainstream activity, not just the purview of the few.

The Thinking Machine

The invention of the computer – the "thinking machine" – was initially heralded as the solution to our problems. The long hoped for "world brain" would enable us to capture all of knowledge in an encyclopedia and access it with the help of an army of indexers. H.G. Wells articulated that vision in 1938. His optimism and certainty about the rosy future technology will bring us is clear:

> *"The whole human memory can be, and probably in a short time will be, made accessible to every individual. And what is of very great importance to this uncertain world where destruction becomes continually more frequent and unpredictable is this, that photography affords now every facility for multiplying duplicates of this – which we may call? – this new all-human cerebrum. It need not be concentrated in any one single place. It need not be vulnerable as a human head or a human heart is vulnerable*

*. . . This is no remote dream, no fantasy. It is a plain statement
of a contemporary state of affairs . . . . It is difficult not to believe
that in the quite near future this Permanent World Encyclopedia,
so compact in its material form and so gigantic in its scope and
possible influence, will not come into existence."[21]*

About the same time, Vannever Bush wrote an article "As We May Think"
(first published after World War II) in which he foresaw the impact of
computers that he and others were beginning to build.

That vision failed . . . as did other visions of a single solution to life's
problems. What has happened, to our surprise, is we have learned that
knowledge and information is based in communities, not in a "world brain."
Knowledge is more than an accumulation of information. Perhaps the most
surprising part of the move of technology into the thinking realm is the
emergence of communities as the location of knowledge.

Communities are where thinking takes place. People are the real
"thinking machines," but their thought, when it becomes thought that is
done to make a living, always takes place in a context – within a community. Information can be taken out of context and brought together with
information from other, sometimes unrelated, places as part of information management. But knowledge always requires a context for it to be
of value. Context is the bridge that links information together and creates
knowledge.

New technologies, especially web technologies such as the internet,
enable people to find information and bring it into a new context, the work
of the knowledge worker. However, most people have been (and still are)
hired to do physical labor – to grow crops, forge steel and move mountains – sometimes mountains of earth and sometimes mountains of paper
work that stream across desks in a bureaucratized society. But even those
who are hired to do physical labor are becoming knowledge workers as
the machines, particularly the computer, take over and rationalize many of
the physical tasks, by making them simpler and more "logical".

Professionals – the modern thinkers

Traditionally, a profession is characterized by the professional's ability to
control the work situation and set fees. Professionals, so the definition goes,

---

[21] Wells. H.G., "A Permanent World Encyclopedia" in World Brain. London: Methuen &
Co, 1938. p. 61.

are those who are free to do their work when, where, and how long they wish. Instead of selling time, which someone else directs, the professional sells the product of thinking. This relationship exists today, most often, for consultants, but even consultants often work for organizations that sell their time, not their products. Relatively few professionals are able to set their own time and place of work. Even doctors, lawyers, psychologists and accountants who once worked as "independent" professionals are part of institutions which determine and shape the work that they do.

One group of professional employees, faculty in universities, was considered to be outside the mainstream of productive society and had a special status in society. Alexander von Humboldt, the inventor of the modern university – described this status as "Einseimkeit und Freiheit" – Loneliness and Freedom. The professor's freedom came from the non-involvement in society and productive work.

With the rise of the modern university, alongside the modern industrial plants in the nineteenth century, jobs for professionals were created by the State (and its close ally the Church). These people were paid to think and provided with a lifetime security (called tenure in a university).

In all walks of life, the numbers of those who do professional work is increasing dramatically. Even though these professionals generally work for institutions; often for very large institutions, they do the work that "independent" professionals once did. Their work is now very much a part of the productive activities of society. They are analysts, scientists, and professionals with a wide variety of titles and responsibilities, all united by an expectation that their judgment is what is important in their work.

The professions each have a common body of knowledge – which infuses and guides their work and the status that they have in society. The body of knowledge grows and is developed through the collaboration of professionals regardless of the places where they work.

"Freetime" – From Vocation to a Job

"Free time" is the time when you don't work. Such a concept was traditionally foreign to the professional. Working time and professional time were intertwined. According to the mythology of the profession, all time belongs to those in the profession – to the calling. The calling infuses all activity whether at the work place or at home – in public or in private – whether you are on or off the job. The professional is always on call and always at work – always thinking. This idealized state is, however, seldom realized by most of those called professionals.

By definition, then, the professional, the thinker, has no free time and no private life, even when that work is done in an industrial setting. The codes of conduct common to most professions bind the professional to constant service. They read more like vows than contracts for the delivery of goods and services.

However, once professionals begin working in the industrial mode, the de-professionalization begins. Private spaces are recognized that enable the professional to have a "personal" life when not at work. Political beliefs, sexual attitudes and practices, and other "private" matters are thought to be irrelevant to the work place.

Some elements of "professional" work survive, even in the industrial mode. Most contracts for professional services exempt professional jobs from certain labor laws such as required payments for overtime. Often professionals are expected to adhere to "ethical" standards which apply only to professionals and not to other workers.

The additional requirements put on professional workers do not diminish the fact that the professional is paid for the time spent on duty, which is under the control of the institution employing the professional.

"De-Professionalization"

The essence of the industrialization process is the establishment of free time and interchangeability.

When workers came to the factory, they were "freed" from their land. Individual workers assumed the responsibility for family, education, health, religion and politics that were previously provided by the communities from which they came. Freedom meant liberation from constraints imposed by what was often a closed society, but it also meant the end of community based support systems.

The peasants were freed from their responsibilities to the social system in which they lived when they assumed their role as a worker within a factory. The skills of the work place became interchangeable and the individual workers could be replaced and substitutes found when one worker wore out or a more qualified or available worker emerged. A similar process occurs as professionals enter the industrial work place.

The subjective manifestation of the transformation of a vocation or calling into a job is alienation – a sense of malaise. A separation and loss of control enters into the life of the professional who becomes a part of the industrial system. But free time does not just mean the separation of work time from free time – it also means that pay and compensation become linked to work time. Instead of allegiance to the "public" and to a code of ethics, the professional contracts with the owner of the means of production and is paid for the time that he or she devotes to the work – or part of that time, most companies expect professional staff to work till the job's done, but be paid for a steady 40 hour week.

Once "free time" becomes ubiquitous, the process of increasing the efficiency of "work time" begins. Once "work time" becomes standardized, efficiency can be easily measured by looking at how long specific tasks take. Prior to the creation of "work time," there is no standard of efficiency – except perhaps a notion of "peer review" or evaluation by peers. A "good idea" may take years ... or only a few minutes, but the quality of an idea cannot be measured by how long it took to produce that idea.

As professionals become part of the work force, this review is replaced either by legal boards and commissions who, with the power of the State, license and certify professional norms. Over time, however, the enforcement of these norms switches from the profession to the institution that employs the professional. Although the norms and standards may be developed within the profession, the enforcement is normally carried out through the work place, not by the profession itself. Managers, who may or may not be part of the same profession, control the work place.

When pay is linked to performance and performance is linked to the amount of time it takes to make the product of thought, then quantification of work can proceed. The linkage of pay to work time also means that the basis is created for conflicts among professionals, now hired for their work time, and the traditional requirement that professionals are "free-standing" thinkers in control of their work.

For the professional, efficiency is antithetical to the entire tradition and, indeed, to the work which needs to be done. Freedom for the thinker is a freedom to work. The thinker requires the right and possibility to associate with other members of the profession and to organize time in accordance with his professional needs, not the needs of the manager in charge of the work place. For the professional to work well, working conditions may be needed that that can run counter to the driving force that brings efficiency, understood as the amount of time it takes to perform a task in the industrial work place.

Professional Associations

All jobs are organized – some by those who do them, more often by those who set up and control the jobs. When we come to look at the concept of community of practice, we shall see that much of the "informal" organization of work takes place by those who do the work, sometimes ignoring the specific directives of management.

Organizing, then, is a fact of all work.

Some organizing, however, is self-organizing – a group of people who come together to pursue common ends. It is one of the forms of organizing that comes out of the socialization of work.

Simply being forced to work together is not enough for organized work to be possible. For decades, a group of people can be forced to work side-by-side on assembly lines and not have any sense they have a common interest with those next to them.

The first form of organization of knowledge workers comes through the professional society. The professional association seeks to manage the value of the knowledge work done by the profession. Sometimes this takes the form of limiting competition in order to preserve the status of those currently in the profession. Other times, it may work to improve the public image of the profession, but in the end, the primary function of a professional organization is to decide who is 'in" and who is "out" of the profession. Self-regulation also enables the association to maintain the standards of the profession, although in practice enforcement is normally left to the employer of the professional, not the organization.

As we noted earlier, a profession shares a body of knowledge. A well-formed body of knowledge is best developed within sciences – such as physics or biology or sociology as well as in some professions, such as law and medicine. Other professions may not have such a clearly defined and accepted "body," but professional organizations and associated education instutitions, seek to establish and maintain a "special" body of knowledge as a characteristic for a profession. A body of knowledge embodies the shared conclusions of a group of people working in a common area. A body of knowledge is generally not located in just one or two places. The members of the community accept certain "repositories" of the knowledge of the community. In the scientific world, these repositories are often scientific journals where the results of research are published. In professions and other disciplines, the bodies of knowledge are gathered together and made accessible through educational and training programs, through trade publications and through regular gatherings of the members of the professions.

In addition to having a body of knowledge, the professional association often endorses, monitors and enforces standards – a quasi-governmental function. The association seeks to write standards which are written into laws and governmental regulations. Associations seek to use their codes of conduct as a means to control entry into the profession, with the assistance of governmental authorities.

Licensing is a governmental activity, often closely linked to professional associations. Licensing confers the approval of government to the association. Sometimes this is done directly by requiring a licensed professional to be certified by a particular organization. Sometimes it is done through requirements that professionals achieve a degree granted by an accredited institution – with the accreditation under the control of the association.

Universities Straddle Conflicting Missions

In the German University, a Chair was occupied by a single scholar – one who had an overview, a command of the entire field. In English Universities, a Don pursued truth as an individual occupation. In the modern university, however, management is in the hands of an administrator of a department of specialists – each one seeking to be increasingly competent in a specific area. The administrator may come from a separate "profession" (that of administration) and oversees professionals who have become workers in highly specialized fields, and have lost the range of vision intellectuals once had.

The independence of institutions where professional work goes on was created to protect the work of the professional from "outside" control. However, this independence was long ago replaced by a close cooperation in the areas of research among government, industry and universities. Universities that were created as research centers are now very much a part of the business world.

The major impetus for the modern university was the rise of the nation state. The university became the institution charged with articulating a culture and establishing and maintaining cultural dominance for the nation. Maintaining a culture is a conserving, restrictive cooperative activity, not an open, creative collaborative activity.

In addition, however, universities, research institutions, and other places of work for professionals are charged with the task of bringing scientific and technical progress to the society. The professional is one more element in the vast machine of industry. In the process, thinking achieves a new historical role within the working process.

The Production of Knowledge

The use of machines, particularly computers, as a precondition for professional work has been going on for many years. In the sciences, this process is already well advanced and research requires elaborate equipment that can only be purchased within an institutional framework. Every phase of activity – including thinking, now takes place within a system of division of labor.

The machine and its software increasingly determine how work is done. Work is organized around the needs of the systems, not the needs of the workers in the industrial mode of production.

The increase in productive power that comes from the interchangeability of labor in an industrialized system is enormous. Knowledge is now truly cumulative in nature, at least in principle. As the work of the industrialized professional moves from cooperation to collaboration, a new work culture begins to emerge.

Knowledge becomes embodied in communities of practice, not just in the work of a great man. The production of knowledge becomes collective.

The Commodity Relationship

Contract law makes it clear that products that are made on work time belong to the person paying for the time, not the person doing the work.

The transformation of professional work into a job was not complete, however, until intellectual work could be bought and sold – and itself become a product of exchange, a commodity. The process of buying and selling intellectual labor time is not fundamentally different from buying and selling other labor time. In order to sell work time, it is codified and quantified so that it can be measured. This requires the work to be rationalized and quantified. The rationalization of intellectual labor takes the same form as other rationalizations in the industrial work place – the elements of the productive process are quantified so that they can be measured. Of course, the essence of intellectual and professional labor runs counter to these forms of "rationalization" – for what "makes sense" to a knowledge worker may be very different from what is required to a speeding up of work processes.

Professional work becomes a commodity once it has value in is own right and can be bought and sold like other commodities. As with other work, the time of the worker is what is sold, and an institutional framework is necessary for the value to be extracted from that time. The worker turns over a certain portion of the day to the person who purchases it.

Commodities have been with us for a long time, but only in the last few centuries has work been organized around managing work time as a commodity. In the industrial mode of production the buying and selling of work-time reaches its full expression. In an industrial form of work, in an industrial workplace, work-time is purchased, pooled with the work-time of other workers, who cooperate in the productive process. Work is brought under the control of a coordinator, a director. This direction can take place at a very high level with managers between the owner and the worker, but control remains in the hands of those who own the means of production, not those who do the work. Someone else in the industrialized setting owns the work of the professional.

A commodity is freely exchanged and can be replaced by another. The specialness that is a part of work done by a professional vanishes in the industrial work place. The work is "freed" from the vagaries of the individual. As a result, the professional, like other workers, is invited to move on to find other work at any time. "If you don't like it here, you can always go somewhere else" assumes that there is somewhere else to go and that professional work can be transferred from one setting to another.

Patents and Copyrights

The patent and copyright laws are the legal system relating to the ownership of intellectual property and the exchange of labor time. These laws were initially established to protect the individual products of thinkers from theft. It was determined, and rightfully so, that someone who had labored for years on particular product should not be robbed of the fruits of that product once it reached fruition.

The products of the individual professionals are registered with the government and the government and the courts enforce the rights of the inventor or the creator.

Once corporations were defined as persons at the turn of the nineteenth century, most copyrights and patents began to be held by artificial entities – corporations, universities and other institutions.

Applying for patents and copyrights became a highly technical process that spawned a support system of patent attorneys.

In the professional work place of buying and selling, those who pay for the labor time of professionals generally own their intellectual property, like other property. Copyright and patent laws that initially were established to reward and protect individual scientists become laws that assure that the institutions receive the benefits of intellectual labor.

The individual professional, in order to work, requires the use of tools and an environment that is often available only in the "thinking factories"

The exchange that the individual makes is to sell the right to his thinking (labor) time and products to the institution.

Only products developed during "free" time are the property of the individual. In fact, only truly independent thinkers do their thinking outside the thinking factories. This is possible, however, only for intellectual work that does not require instructional support, laboratory equipment, sophisticated machinery, or the collaboration of other thinkers.

The final link between the market place and the professional comes in research and development – where the thinker, the new product and the market place come together. In research and development, the individual scientist, working in the laboratory is progressively transformed into a part of the corporate life. The creation of research and development as a specific activity with specific funding as a part of universities, the government, and major corporations unites thinking and practice.

In the past, the link between theory and practice was a mediated one – the people who did the theory did not worry about the practical implementation of their work.

With research and development, however, the link becomes direct.

Buying and Selling Professional Time

Now that most professionals work in organizations, they are not, as they once were, isolated and lonely individuals on the periphery of society. They are an important part of the productive work force. In the Knowledge Age, thinkers (professionals) become more and more important.

Once the process of buying and selling professional labor is institutionalized and professional labor-time is treated like other commodities, the work of the professional is brought under the same control as the work of other workers. A high level of cooperation is expected from these workers, like other workers.

As the professionals identify primarily with the employer, rather than colleagues who do not share the same work place, teamwork is praised and promoted. Cooperation becomes an important value for professionals in the industrial work place. Even though teamwork is praised, collaboration, once a normal activity of professionals, is often discouraged, at least collaboration with those outside the employing company. The professional becomes an important property of the company. Contacts beyond the realm of the company need to be organized and controlled for the benefit of the company.

The result is that in the individual work place, the work of the professional is closely identified with an institution, not with a community that shares a profession.

The impact on the nature of work – once the commodity process is imposed on professional work is fundamental. In earlier models of intellectual work, the family model prevailed – for example, the doctoral "father" or the dissertation adviser served as the tutor and assisted the young scholar to enter the life of the mind. Like a parent, the scholar directed the work but received no value other than the satisfaction of watching a child grow and mature. The scholar as a parent is still found in some recesses of intellectual work places. However, once the commodity relationship is established, the professional takes on a managerial role, not a nurturing role, to those who work with and for him or her.

Management

The rise of the professional manager requires the development of tools to organize the work of the professional. These include certification (in conjunction with professional associations), codes of ethics and contracts that ensure that the intellectual products are the property of the company, not the professional. With these tools, the manager, not the professional, is able to manage the work place.

When thought becomes industrialized, work takes on a different character. The activity of thinking must fit into a productive process and be pieced together with the work of others. Research and development go hand in hand. Thought, once it is a productive activity, becomes a valuable product. The value of work is determined by the employer. The control of the work place passes from the professional to the manager and pressures abound to constantly increase the efficiency of the production. The work of the professional in an industrialized setting lacks the elements of self-direction that make professional work self-fulfilling and were once essential to the definition of professional work.

In traditional professions, control of the profession is vested with those involved in the activity – either individually or collectively. There are no bosses. But in the new order, the bosses of intellectuals need not be intellectuals nor even understand what thinkers do, any more than the bosses of industrial workers need to be familiar with the work that is being done.

The industrialization of professions creates managers of thought. A professional manager is appointed whose job it is to run and supervise the thinking activity.

Initially, at least, the heads of large departments of professionals may be professionals. The management function, it is thought, is one that requires a particular knowledge of the activity of the workers. Soon, however we see the development of a managing profession – the hospital administrator, the higher education administrator, etc.

For example, at universities the president and other members of the administration were once faculty members who assumed the post for a limited time and then returned to the faculty. Now, however, administration becomes its own activity, with its own specialized knowledge and the link between the community of scientific enquirers and the managers of that knowledge is broken.

The problem with professional managers, especially in areas where knowledge is produced, is that they need to know enough about the activities to determine if they are being done correctly, at least when they are called upon to manage knowledge workers.

With the industrialization of thinking as a job activity, disciplines emerge with specific knowledge domains. Job descriptions are devised, evaluation systems put in place, and work becomes ordered as the tools created by human resource managers for industrial settings are applied to professions. The disciplining of work then begins in earnest as work is quantified, divided and sub-divided until the professional often no longer understands what is going on – just as the artisan was replaced by the factory workers who soon lost any appreciation and understanding of the totality of the work.

The professional manager is the implementer of the desires and wishes (the policies) of those who own the institutions where intellectual work takes place, not the professionals who work there.

Financial rewards follow the managers, not the professionals, while the ultimate benefits of professional labor go to the owners of the firm. Managerial functions for professional activities and institutions were once considered to be "clerk-like" functions of a lower status. Some positions were rotated among the professionals, but few professionals had a goal of becoming a manager. As managers began to be paid more than professionals, however, the ranks of professional administrators grew rapidly as they sacrificed their relationship to the work place and assumed managerial functions.

The manager in the thinking factory, just as the manager in other factories, is given one job – to get maximum production at the least cost. The manager is required not only to see that production breaks even, but also that the production increases as time goes on.

The test of a good manager is how much production he can get from the workforce in the least amount of time. For professionals, like other workers, pressures mount to become "productive" and to increase productivity. "Incompetent" and "unproductive" workers and managers are weeded out. Everything is bought, sold and quantified. The thrust of the productive process is to bring order where chaos and individual direction once dominated.

Once professional workers are brought under control, they must cooperate in order for production to go on. And in this cooperation lies the possibility for a new – and different – way to do work. Cooperative work begins to develop a new work culture – a culture that can lead to collaboration as an essential aspect of knowledge work.

Knowing More and More About Less and Less

In the industrial setting, the individual thinker is expected to know more and more about less and less.

General knowledge becomes a matter of interdisciplinary activity, rather than an understanding of the totality of reality. Interdisciplinary work, by its very nature, is cooperative in character and scope. Cooperation develops as experts from various fields attack overlapping work. Specialists, each of whom knows a particular field or part of a field very well, cooperate to produce a particular product. Cooperation of this kind requires a manager to bring together the disparate specialists. In this sense, the precondition of interdisciplinary activity is the division of labor.

Division of labor and the cooperative work that comes with it transforms many professionals into coordinators and managers, while other professionals are absorbed into the "paraprofessional" group of workers. A laboratory becomes identified as the property of the head of the laboratory – just as the Carnegie steel mill was identified as the personal property of the owner of the plant.

Within the laboratory, just as within the plant, many professionals become managers. Instead of doing work themselves, they become directors of teams of technicians. They find satisfaction through the work of others, not their own work.

But the division of labor does not stop here – for managing itself becomes a specialty. Professional administrators emerge who take over the control of the work process. In the end, nothing is left. The work that once centered on an individual may be divided among a team. Cooperation replaces individual labor.

To be done well, knowledge work – the work of the professionals – requires more than cooperation. It requires collaboration, which is the key characteristic of the work culture that is most appropriate for knowledge work. We shall look further into the distinction between cooperation and collaboration in the next chapter.

Manual and Intellectual Labor

Much knowledge work is very physical in nature. Knowledge work does not mean "not physical." In fact, knowledge work often combines physical activity and intellectual work.

The emergence of knowledge work and the collaborative work culture that best enables knowledge work to be done well brings with it a number of surprising changes in how we view work.

One of these is the elimination of a strict distinction between manual and intellectual labor. The "blue collar" worker is becoming professionalized and the "white collar" worker is becoming industrialized.

These two processes converge to produce a new kind of work in which physical tasks are, whenever possible, automated out of existence or replaced by machines and intellectual tasks require an understanding and participation in the work process.

We turn now to the consideration of the contradictions that arise as professionals become workers and workers become professionals. We turn to an examination of the conditions for the new work culture.

CHAPTER 3

From Cooperation to Collaboration

How we do our work is mostly a matter of habit. These habits are developed, over a period of time in response to the needs of the work place and the tools (technologies) that are available to get the work done. The development of knowledge work as the primary kind of work means we will need new habits to get the work done efficiently and well. Developing these habits requires a transformation of the work culture, for the work culture is made up of the beliefs and expectations that we bring to our work.

As we shall see later, an integrated digital environment, along with communities of practice and knowledge work, gives us a way to think about the new culture of work, the culture appropriate to knowledge work, which is being created. Before we go to those concepts, we need to look closer at the difference between cooperation and collaboration – the key difference between a work culture in an industrialized setting and a work culture for knowledge work to thrive.

Beliefs That Underlie the New Work Culture

Knowledge work is:

- inherently collaborative
- not bound by space and time

- done by collaborating teams
- done in an environment in which information is shared, not hoarded
- customer/client centered
- driven from below, not managed from above

The characteristics of the work culture of an integrated digital environment are:

1. Trust

In a trusting work relationship, work is done in a transparent work environment. People "know" one another, even if they have never met. They can determine the value of the knowledge that others produce – the information they use to do their work. The work done and the roles played need to be understood and accepted (not just acquiesced to). The manager trusts that the information used by the subordinate (which is available to the manager at all times) is the latest and most accurate available. The subordinate trusts that his/her data/information are accepted as authoritative.

2. Collaboration

Immediate access to information needed to do work requires collaborative relationships in which each person with a need to know has access to another's work without the owner having to post his/her work and without the seeker gaining access via special permission.

3. Preservation of and Access to Essential Evidence

A corporate memory system preserves the evidence created in doing work so that it can be re-used by others.

The change in our work culture is already well underway. What will it be like?

Information Sharing

Information sharing is the key to successful collaboration in doing knowledge work, because the knowledge that I make in the course of doing knowledge work becomes someone else's information that they need to do their work.

Sometimes the sharing that goes on is individual in nature. More often, however, it goes beyond that – it comes out of working together in a community or communities to accomplish a goal – to do work.

We have all, from time to time, been fortunate enough to experience true collaboration. The difference between collaboration and cooperation is the difference between playing a team sport and simply playing at the same time. Cooperation is like what psychologists call parallel play in which two or more kids play side by side, but aren't necessarily playing the same "game." They may share and cooperate while each playing his or her own game. Sometimes (and this is often a function of age), however, the children begin to share in a game. It is no longer this person's game or that person's game. The game belongs to everyone who plays, regardless of the particular role they assume. Collaboration is a creative process that emerges out of a common desire to achieve a goal. Collaboration takes place when we all play the same game, with the same goals and a common understanding of what the game is about.

One way to understand collaboration is to look at the community of people who make up a sports team. There are players, a coach, a statistician, the announcer and fans. Some of the players are stars and others often spend their time sitting on the bench. But all of these community members are members of the team. More than cooperation is necessary for a team to succeed. "Team spirit" is characteristic of successful team play. The "spirit" is sometimes described in mystical terms – and when we are fortunate to play on a really good team – even if our play is merely sitting on the bench watching the stars perform – we are filled with a kind of awe and surprise and satisfaction that comes from a job well done. We are part of the team, regardless of the particular role that we might play.

In the Age of Knowledge, the work culture is driven by the need to access information in order to create knowledge. Such access depends on the collaboration of other team members. We work in communities where we have sharing relationships with those who create the information we need to do our work. If we are fortunate, we will work in good teams where "team spirit" pervades our environment.

We are beginning to imagine and experience new ways of doing work that were once not even thinkable. When we work in the web, we can make our work accessible to others. They can simply "look over our shoulder" and see the latest results of our work.

We can achieve that degree of intimacy and trust within a community – one whose environment is cared for and nurtured in such ways that trust is established. Knowledge work flourishes when we know one another and we know how to evaluate the work others are doing with us, when the information others produce is available to us and helps us do our work efficiently and with confidence.

Changing the assumptions people bring to their work is not a simple, or a one-time, activity. Sometimes work cultures change imperceptibly over time because of introduction of new tools. Sometimes change comes because of a dramatic (and not always welcome) disruption – a bankruptcy, a take-over by another company, war or civil unrest.

Change comes from many places. It can also be planned and managed. We can learn from others how change is accomplished, but the process itself must grow out of a work place with a vision of the possibilities for new ways of doing work. We can identify as least three important elements to managing change:

- Be clear about what we want. Have a vision and understanding of where we are going and what our real work is . . . and what is achievable.
- Provide leadership. Show the way. Set the example and reward those who follow it.
- Empower the knowledge workers by establishing performance based learning and creating a favorable technological environment.

Predicting and steering a change in work culture is not as important as embracing it and welcoming it. We shall speak later about how such a work culture comes about – about how transformation comes one person at a time.

When an organization understands and articulates clearly its real work (its mission), when the leadership is dedicated to providing the tools and policies that make immediate access to information possible for the workers, and when workers share and are rewarded for sharing information with their community; then transformation is afoot.

The Fourth Wave

The Knowledge Age is the "Fourth Wave." Work in the Age of Knowledge is, as we said before, largely the production of knowledge. As we enter this Knowledge Age, our work takes on very different characteristics than the work we do in an industrial environment. In this new age, in order for work to be done most efficiently, we will not be paid for our work time . . . but for what we know and what we get done.

The Fourth Wave

The term "fourth wave" was first used, we believe, by Herb Schantz. He took Toffler's notion of the "third wave"(the information age) and says that the information age is just a transition to the knowledge age. The first wave is agricultural, the second industrial and the third, the information age. We believe that the information (computer) age is the last stage in the industrial age . . . and the transition to the knowledge age. It is not particularly important how we name and number these "ages" – the point is that fundamental changes seem to be occurring. So many parts of our lives are changing so dramatically that it makes sense of a "new age." It is hard to tell, particularly at the beginning of such an age, if it is really new. But the evidence is pretty well in . . . making knowledge is really quite different from other kinds of work.

We are at the beginning of that Age – an Age as different from the Computer Age (sometimes called the Information Age) as the Industrial Age was from the Manufacturing Age and the Manufacturing Age from the Agrarian Age. The Computer/Information Age is the final stage of the industrial age, for it applies automation to tasks that were once thought to be uniquely human. Work, including much of the work of the professionals, is rationalized, channeled, and brought within an industrialized structure.

The function of technology is often to eliminate manual work . . . to simply make some physical activities no longer necessary. Work process improvement focuses on these issues . . . how to stop doing what we used to do, particularly the stuff we called work; particularly the stuff that bored us, the stuff machines can now do. The Knowledge Age is made possible by new technologies properly applied and by integrating technologies in such a way that they encourage knowledge sharing within and among communities.

Computers and wires do not improve work, but they provide the possibility of making improvements. The technologies that enable knowledge work were among the first products of the Information Age, which, we argued, is the end phase of the Industrial Age, an age driven by many heady new inventions, and machines. Work and knowledge come together in the Knowledge Age. Putting the terms knowledge and work together enables us to begin to think about the transformation of work and culture needed to support knowledge work.

Consciously Changing a Work Culture

When our work is to make knowledge, we need to be free from the constraints of time . . . and selling our time. We need to focus on doing what "makes sense," what is appropriate in a particular time and context within a particular community.

As we move into the collaborative world, we invent new kinds of "offices" that enable us to communicate with others much more efficiently than when we had to meet at the same time and place. "Meetings" are replaced by collaborative activities – by discussions and interchange.

Information transfer, one of the primary reasons for meetings in the industrial mode of production, is done much more efficiently through web-based working environments, where those involved in a project can look over the shoulder of their colleagues without disturbing their work and get the latest and best available information.

The trusting relationship required for this relationship is one of the primary characteristics of the new work culture. Trust can be measured and observed. Trust here is not a "moral" trust in the honesty of another, but simply the assurance that the information accessible is the best available information at any given time. My colleague, Evie Lotze, in her companion book to this one, Work Culture Transformation, gives a tool to observe and give a qualitative measurement to the existence of the beliefs that underlie the new work culture.

A new work culture is, at least in part, a new way to think about things – a new set of expectations, a new "common sense" about work. This new way of thinking develops out of old ways, often through and by thinkers who developed ideas and concepts that help us know and understand what is happening in our life.

The application of spiral thinking (we will speak much more about this later) to solve practical problems on a wide scale is relatively new. We can see, in nearly every field, some kind of agile, spiral thinking proposed.

A collaborative and information-sharing work culture readily adapts to change. Change brings in fresh ideas, allows for and promotes creativity and flexibility. Knowledge work is too dynamic for assembly line planning and execution. Knowledge creation itself embodies change.

Collaborative and information sharing work environments are flexible in nature and maintain clear communication paths over extended durations. In a collaborative environment, flux is the norm.

New technologies bring with them possibilities for new work cultures – but culture has a way of lingering and shaping the way we live. Common sense is built and shaped to enable us to survive the way we work.

Transforming a work culture requires creating a new "common sense" that is appropriate for knowledge work.

It is possible to consciously change a work culture. Convincing people to change their minds and attitudes (although that is important) is not enough. Neither is it a matter of simply introducing new machines into the work place. It requires a new way of thinking accompanied by tools appropriate for knowledge work.

Change, including culture change, can be fostered, if not managed. A body of theory and practice relating to change management has grown up over the years. The name "change management" often implies that someone else's culture changes. True culture change means that the culture of the leader must change as well – the leader is not just the encourager or the one who mandates that others change. Leadership in culture transformation is best done by example.

Transforming a work culture requires changing the shared attitudes toward work, the shared beliefs and the common expectations about behavior, etc. In the industrial world, the machine determined and drove that work culture and the owner of the machines coordinated the work.

The emergence of the knowledge age brings with it a new work culture. Creating a new work culture, is all about integration – integrating people with disparate ideas into collaborating communities of practice, bringing together apparently disparate trends from different fields and melding them into a whole. Much has been written about managing change, about technology, about leadership, about responses to change and about management in the new environment. Our focus is on integrating concepts from a variety of disciplines into new concepts that guide and inform the transformation. We will integrate some familiar concepts into new concepts – terms with a twist that create a new way of thinking about transforming work.

Two Definitions of Culture

Culture: "all that is nonbiological and socially transmitted in a society" – Charles Inick, Dictionary of Anthropology. Philosophical Library. 1956. p. 144

Culture: "The accumulated store of symbols, ideas and material products associated with a social system, whether it be an entire society or a family . . . . Culture does not refer to what people actually do, but to the ideas they share about what they do and the material objects they use." All Johnson, Blackwell Dictionary of Sociology. 1995 p. 68

These integrating concepts embody a new way of thinking . . . a new culture that develops in a non-linear way – a holistic view of the world that is spiral in nature.

This spiral development is sometimes referred to as a positive feedback cycle by systems thinkers. In this world, information sharing replaces information hoarding. We collaborate and create knowledge out of information. We have new assumptions about what we do and how we spend our time. All this, taken together, is culture change, or work transformation.

Our work is becoming knowledge work. Everyday life is being transformed underneath the veneer of sameness. But the work is changing and many people are beginning to adopt very different ways to relate to their work.

Let's explore some of the differences between the two work cultures, the industrial mode and the knowledge mode.

Work Cultures Old and New

The work culture of the Industrial Age	The work culture of the Knowledge Age
Cooperation	Collaboration
Information hoarding	Information Sharing
Managers organize our work	We organize our work time and place as appropriate for the job to be done.
We are paid for the time we are at work	We are paid to acquire knowledge, think, and make good decisions.
We come to work and when we are not working, we have free time.	Thinking cannot be turned on and off.

Industrialization – and the work culture that grew up to support industrialization permeated the farm, the factory, the office, the artisan shop as work was brought under the discipline of machines. Manufacturing brought people together in large urbanized settings to do work they once did in isolated situations. With the introduction of power (initially steam) and machines to drive the process, the nature of work changed and gave rise to what is called the industrial revolution – an age that divided work into progressively small pieces of efficiency.

The industrial revolution brought with it a new kind of work culture, one built on the principle that:

- work time is a commodity that can be managed
- production is a matter of using less and less work time to make more and more products.

The knowledge revolution brings with it new ways of thinking about work and production. The move from cooperation to collaboration is the key step in making a work culture for knowledge work.

Moving From Cooperation to Collaboration

Cooperation, which is highly developed in the industrial mode of production, fosters an attitude of control. Information is power. Those who have information control power. By cooperating, I trade with you what you need to do your task. The sharing is only for a limited time and some kind of "return" is expected. Cooperation is also essential for the assembly line to function. Everything depends on each person doing his or her job well and efficiently – so that one piece can move on so the next worker can do his or her part of the assembly.

Collaboration, on the other hand, requires that people understand what others are doing and how their work fits together with the work of others. It also requires a much higher level of inter-dependency for success in the work than cooperative environments do. Collaboration is a win-win situation because all those involved have a common goal.

Cooperation is about negotiating – giving people enough to make them go away. Collaboration is about developing networks and connections and common goals. Collaboration involves trust.

In the Industrial Age, the quantification of labor into labor time means that work loses its connection to the product being produced and, instead, is linked to the amount of time that is put into making that product. This separation of the worker from the products of work is called alienated labor – work that becomes foreign to the person producing labor.

Figure I

Cooperation – Industrial Work	Collaboration – Knowledge Work
Information is traded.	Work is done in work groups that coalesce and disband.
Division of labor. Tasks are divided and parceled out.	The worker needs to understand the totality of the work being done.
The worker does not understand all that is going on.	Collaboration requires relatively small, but intertwined communities.
Work and workers are brought together into large enterprises.	Knowledge work is about production, about applying force (thought, research, creativity) to information and moving it a distance toward the goal, mission, vision so that something is changed or transformed. Results and quality, not speed and quantity, determine efficiency.
Cost/Benefit analysis enables the cost that goes into a product or products to be measured against the margins generated.	
Productivity increased by automating tasks and improving work flow.	
Automation enables machines to take over more and more of the tasks that we do. Automation frees us from the routine.	Productivity increased by increasing communication and integrating work.
Efficiencies flow from increasing the scale of production in order to decrease costs and write off the expenses of automation.	Automation enables work; it does not take it over.
	Efficiencies flow from doing work within communities united by a shared body of knowledge so that knowledge is accessible and dependable when needed.
Industrialization advances by the simplification of complex tasks so that interchangeable workers can perform them. By dividing labor into discreet tasks, these tasks lose their artistic character and become interchangeable.	Standards arise out of the work that is done. They are rules/conventions/ norms adopted for communication among communities in order to make information accessible.
Managers control and direct projects with specified stages from beginning to end. Management focuses on meeting production goals, keeping people in their proper places and coordinating the work of hundreds or thousands of people.	People work in communities and come together to accomplish particular tasks and accomplish work with a shared goal. Work is done together. Collaborative work is done together.

The chain of command drives the increase in production.	Collaboration is an organic process and, like most things organic, is not hierarchical, neatly channeled and managed.
The work force works side-by-side with communications channeled through appropriate hierarchies.	
The industrial mode of production brings people together in a place and organizes them around machines that determine how work is done. These places may be factories or offices. The essential determination of work is the machine – its demands and its needs.	The relationship to the customer – the user of the products needs to be as direct as possible, because it is the needs of the user that determines the work that is done.
	Knowledge work does not require gathering people together in order to do work. People continue to come together for work and pleasure, but the driving force of the machine is replaced by the need for a collaborative and nurturing environment.
Cooperation comes from workers whose work is aligned by management to achieve the purposes and goals of the enterprise. Each member of the team must cooperate with others. A production line is perhaps the best example of a cooperative work environment in the industrial society. People work side-by-side, with work processes organized and controlled by management to assure maximum productivity.	Collaboration is not just among individuals, but institutes, laboratories, departments and work teams. Collaboration involves doing work together, depending on one another, not just cooperating so each individual work gets done.
Cooperation requires accepting and following work rules prescribed by management.	Thinking is inherently critical and evaluative – questioning how things have always been done.

Division of labor means that the individual work can only be done cooperatively under the direction of a manager. And yet to do this work well, knowledge workers need to control labor through collaboration in a new work environment. **The work culture needs to facilitate collaboration and move beyond cooperation**.

Cooperation directed by managers gives way to collaboration in those situations in which work is done together. The development of collaborative tools in the digital environment enables collaboration to be done without physical proximity.

Figure 2

A Management View

In 1995 Edward M. Marshall made many of the same points made
in this chapter in a study published by the American Management
Association. He states that "American business is undergoing its most
profound transformation since the Industrial Revolution. . . .
Hierarchy, the cultural principle by which we have led and managed
business for at least the past century no longer seems practical or
relevant."[22] (p. 1)

He goes on to identify the need for "a shared cultural framework
that will be powerful enough to replace hierarchy."[23]

Marshall identifies seven values in what he calls the "collaborative
work ethic," which he proposes to replace the hierarchical work
ethic.

These values are:

Value 1: Respect for people.

"In such an environment, management shifts its role from one of
authority, telling, controlling, and monitoring, to one of facilitating,
coaching, mentoring, and counseling; there is no 'boss.'"[24]

Value 2: Honor and Integrity.

"Because people are interdependent, we need to trust each other,
which means I must believe in others' integrity."[25]

Value 3: Ownership and Alignment.

"The true owners of the organization reside in its workplace . . . By
increasing their stake in its success, the managers can do nothing but
gain. Equally important is the value of alignment that is driven by a

---

[22] Marshall, Edward M. Transforming the Way we Work. The Power of the Collaborative
Workplace. New York: American Management Association. 1995, p. 1.

[23] Ibid., pp. 3–4.

[24] Ibid. p. 29.

[25] Ibid., p. 30.

high level of ownership . . . So, if ownership is the rocket booster, alignment is the guidance system . . . . Alignment occurs when all the members of an organization agree on the vision, mission, and strategic course of action for the company or organization."[26]

Value 4: Consensus

"Many people confuse consensus with compromise or "I can live with it" – as in "I can tolerate that decision." . . . True collaboration requires that individuals in a group responsible for an outcome work *through* their differences.[27]

Value 5: Trust-Based Relationships.

"In the networked organization, authority no longer works as the basis for work relationships. Trust is the new glue."[28]

Value 6: Full Responsibility and Accountability.

"The success of the Collaborative Workplace is most likely to occur when we can move away from the view of responsibility and accountability as being a policing function grounded in a top-down approach to relationships. Instead, we must move toward a view that full responsibility and accountability are horizontal, shared, and grounded in our individual and collective integrity as adults and professionals."[29]

Value 7: Recognition and Growth

"It needs to be okay for people to make some mistakes, to take risks, to try new things, and to learn and grow."[30] (p. 35)

Even though Marshall speaks of values, the language of morality and ethics, his argument is purely practical and business-based. The Collaborative Workplace is the one that works best to get business done.

Collaborative Workplace is the one that works best to get business done.

---

[26] Ibid., p.31.
[27] Ibid, pp. 31–32.
[28] Ibid., p. 32.
[29] Ibid., p. 35.
[30] Ibid.

Measuring Work

If you can't measure the transformation, nothing is known to have happened. How far did the wall move? What difference does it make? A transformation of the work culture is evidenced by observed change in behavior – in this case, from an information-hoarding to an information-sharing environment. Measurements can be qualitative and quantitative.

The measurement of a transformation in work culture serves several purposes. It assures those who are supporting the transformation (your bosses, the public, and your customers) that something is really happening. Even more important, though, is that measurement keeps us in line . . . . and let's us know if we are really doing the work of transformation or merely making an effort. Remember, without results, no work happens.

The industrial mode of production relies heavily on quantitative measurement, as work is parceled out and coordinated.

The measurement of a transformation in the work environment and in the work culture requires more than tracking and measuring the amount of automation. If done properly, the work culture transformation will increase overall productivity in terms of real work. The incentive for work culture transformation comes primarily from improved productivity and quality of work. Quantitative metrics will continue to play an important role in measuring work process improvements that come from applying technology to the solution of problems. As knowledge work moves to the center stage qualitative measurements of productive become more important.

The transformation of a work culture is primarily qualitative in nature . . . it is a different way to approach what we do. It is more than an improvement in *how* we work . . . it is a new way of doing our work – a transformation.

Most psychological and social scientists understand that not everything can or should be quantified. There are other kinds of measurements we can use to determine the nature of the culture in which we live . . . and how that culture is changing. We can observe behavior and from behavior, we can begin to make judgments. In an environment suitable for knowledge work, we can see to what extent a trusting relationship is established, whether information is shared, rather than hoarded and whether the corporate memory is preserved for re-use.

Culture change is qualitative. Once information is accessible, new, collaborative, ways to do that work emerge. Once we define our current work processes, make our products immediately accessible to others and their products accessible to our community, then the transformations in work processes are possible. New attitudes and new assumptions inform our work – we have a work culture based on information sharing.

Overcoming Bad Habits

Creating this new work culture will require us to get a new set of habits – some good and some bad. "Good" and "bad" habits do not refer to moral characteristics, but to which ones are effective or ineffective in a given situation. When we say that these habits are "bad" for knowledge work we mean those habits impede the functioning of communities.

We have spoken above about the new and improved beliefs and attitudes that promote collaboration. But in order to nurture communities, we need to overcome some bad (inhibiting) habits:

- We are taught in school that we need to do our "own" work – that collaborating is cheating.
- We hoard our knowledge
- We don't trust each other or the knowledge another created
- We think information is power, so we hold it close.

These habits are "bad" because they support another way to do work . . . work in the industrial mode. They were/are appropriate for manufacturing and industrial work – work that can be divided, automated and managed centrally. And these habits serve us well when we work in the industrial mode. The same habits impede the development of knowledge work.

It is also true that the "good" habits for knowledge work that we discussed above are also good in a moral sense. When work is properly organized, the alienation inherent in the industrial mode of production is not inherent in knowledge production. In fact, knowledge work requires, for it to be done well, a sense of engagement and ownership – of sharing and working together. These are, we believe, far more satisfying (and productive) ways to work than industrial work.

As collaborative work becomes predominant, we will need to consciously seek to re-use information rather than create new information. This attitude can bring great increases in productivity because information, unlike other resources, grows in value as it is used.

SECTION II

New Ways to Think About Work

In which we consider some new ways to think about work in the Knowledge Age.

Concepts that were once quite separate . . . like "knowledge" and "work" and "community" and "practice" come together to make "knowledge work" and "community of practice." The terms "integrated, "digital" and "environment" are put together as integrated digital environment. These three new concepts for the Knowledge Age

Work is purposeful activity that yields a product of value. Knowledge is a justified true belief. Knowledge work is work that yields a judgment that something is true. It is the answer to the question, "Is it a good idea to . . . ?"

A community is a social institution based on common interests and activity. Practice is the work done based on a shared body of knowledge. A community of practice is the forum in which knowledge work is done.

An integrated digital environment is an environment where there is immediate access to information needed to do work.

The new concepts of Knowledge Work, Community of Practice, and integrated Digital Environment enable us to conceptualize and understand the new culture that is developing in the Knowledge Age.

Key Terms *. (See Glossary for more)*

Community – Groups of people who work for a common purpose within an organization or across organizational boundaries.

Community of practice – A group of people bound together by a common class of problems, common pursuit of solutions, and a store of common knowledge and understanding.

Intcgratcd digital cnvironmcnt – A work environment in which there is immediate access to the information needed to conduct business (to do work).

Praxis (Practice) – The "business" lawyers and doctors maintain; it comprehends all their clients and all the work they do for their clients, including customs and cultural content.

CHAPTER 4

Knowledge Work

So what is knowledge work? It is a kind of work. Like all work we do for a living, knowledge work is of value to someone else – so we are paid for our work. We exchange our valuable work for money.

Of course, much work today does not require thinking, but as automation continues, menial labor is being replaced by thinking labor. Also, of course, we don't get paid every time that we think. We have hobbies. We muse and we volunteer our thinking. But to be knowledge work, it must be both work and require thinking. And to do knowledge work for a living, then it needs to be of value to someone else who pays you to do that work.

Knowledge work is the work of those who think for a living. It is what professionals do. It is what a properly motivated Wal-Mart employees do. It is what scientists do. Obviously the work of Wal-Mart employees and the work of scientists are very different. They have different missions and purposes. Their products are dramatically different. And they come from very different cultures and traditions. But they are all paid to think.

In this section we shall explore concepts that have arisen in the discussion of knowledge management and knowledge work. These concepts help us understand the nature of knowledge work. These concepts come from different disciplines and traditions, but, taken together, they supply us with a vocabulary and some traditions that can give us a fuller understanding of the transformation of work to the knowledge age.

In the next chapters we shall talk about communities of practice, a term developed by anthropologists and educational theorists that focuses on the cultural aspects of an environment for knowledge work. Following that we shall look at the notion of an integrated digital environment – a term used by technologists to describe the technologies and infrastructure that is needed to do work in a digital environment.

The theory of knowledge management that is developing recognizes that knowledge work is the practice of making knowledge explicit. Knowledge work has quite different characteristics from other work. It is, at its very heart, collaborative in nature. Knowledge work is the practice of making knowledge explicit. It:

• Is inherently social. It takes place within a community and calls upon the resources and products of other individuals and communities.
• Makes something new. Creative work (of which knowledge work is one kind) is not simply a matter of inputs and outputs (although there are inputs and outputs). It is a matter of "making" something new – something which did not exist before. For the knowledge worker this is normally a judgment, a conclusion that rises to the point of certainty in the mind of the people doing the work.
• Is of value to someone – an employer or a community.
• Has the characteristics of a spiral. Practice/praxis does not move "logically"[31] from step to step . . . in fact, it relies on inspiration, noticing connections, analyzing, identifying what is important and returning with a new product through the process.
• Has an unpredictable outcome. The goal and purpose of the work can (and should) be identified in advance, but the answer to the question or questions that give rise to knowledge work is not known in advance. If it were, then the process could be automated and a machine could (and should) do that work.

Putting the terms "knowledge" and "work" together does not give us a term that is intuitively understandable. In fact, it is a new concept . . . one that is just now beginning to be used widely. As the term "knowledge work" becomes a part of our language, it provides us a way to bring together what were once thought to be very different activities – doing work and having knowledge.

---

[31] Though, as we shall see, the philosopher Charles Sanders Peirce would say that it is the highest form of logic – that of abduction – used in scientific enquiry. Knowledge work is not purely an inductive or deductive process.

Knowledge workers are those who create knowledge by taking data and information and applying their own experience, judgment, know-how, assumptions (culture), background, and values in order to reach a conclusion. When this is done for a living, these conclusions need to have value for someone else – who is willing to pay them. They know what they do; they are professionals in their field. And they do what they know.

Knowledge is a reasoned conclusion. Knowledge is relevant information embedded in experience that is readily available in a timely manner for users to make timely, valid decisions that increase the productivity of a set of work processes. Knowledge work has value to someone or some community.

No amount of information or data will answer the question, "Is it a good idea to . . . ?" But data and information may be required in order to help us answer the question properly. Data and information are some of the evidence that we use to justify our beliefs. The synergy of information and analysis brings about the answer to the question and produces the knowledge.

Knowledge: Justified True Belief

Knowledge is a good and elevated word. Philosophers have chewed on it for centuries and have, at least in the Western philosophical tradition, come to the conclusion that it is "justified true belief." Philosophers, more than any other folks, worry about knowledge – what it is and how to acquire it. They call that discipline epistemology – the theory of knowledge."

Charles Sanders Peirce on Knowledge

In the 1901 edition of Baldwin's Dictionary of Philosophy and Psychology, C.S. Peirce defines knowledge as follows:

"This word is used in logic in two senses:

(1) as a synonym for Cognition, and

(2) more usefully, to signify a perfect cognition, that is, cognition fulfilling three conditions:

(a) that it holds a proposition that really is true.

(b) that it is perfectly self-satisfied and free from uneasiness of doubt

(c) that some character of this satisfaction is such that it would be logically impossible that this character should ever belong to satisfaction in a proposition not true." (5.605)

Knowledge = Justified True Belief

"Since Plato, nearly all Western philosophers have accepted this deceptively simple statement of the three necessary (and jointly sufficient) conditions for knowledge. That is, I know if and only if: "I sincerely affirm the proposition, The proposition is true, and My affirmation is genuinely based upon its truth." http://noesis.evansville.edu/bin/index.cgi

---

To say that you know something is to make a sincere affirmation of a proposition. Maybe you believe something because some authority (like your mother or a priest) tells you it is true. Or maybe you believe something because you experience it yourself. The "empiricists" – the kind of philosophy that most folks in the United States carry around with them, believe that knowledge is what you experience . . . and if you haven't experienced it you cannot really "know" what you are talking about. Or you might believe something as a product of doing knowledge work – synthesizing, comparing, judging, eliminating and coordinating. In this process, your belief grows because you are able to justify, to provide evidence for, what you believe. Justified beliefs are, generally at least, more valuable than unjustified beliefs. For a belief to be knowledge, it must be justified (or justifiable) by some kind of evidence. Not all beliefs are justified. In fact, we might think that something we used to believe is justified later turns out to be wrong. There is nothing wrong about changing one's mind if there is evidence that leads us to a new belief.

A belief is a conclusion you come to – for some reason or for no reason at all. Some beliefs may be better than others – and in the realm of knowledge work, what separates the good beliefs from the not so good beliefs is the justification that can be given to support the belief.

A "body of knowledge" is the result of lots and lots of experiments, discussions, disputes and examination of evidence that leads to conclusions – conclusions that, taken together, become a "body of knowledge." That is what we learn when we go to school or to training – which beliefs are justified and (if it is good training), why it is justified. As we shall see in the next chapter, a "body of knowledge" is created by and sustained by a community of practice.

Whether or not the world changes, our knowledge of the world does change. Knowledge changes over time, sometimes because the world changes, but more often because we gain new knowledge – justifications for new beliefs. At any given time we are quite certain that what we believe is correct. We have to be certain of our knowledge before we act. We build bridges. We practice medicine. We dance. We make ball bearings. In order to *do* something, we need to *know* something. Knowledge enables us to act. Knowledge enables work.

Notice that we sometimes say something like "I used to believe "x"" "Now I know I was wrong, and I know "y."" Present knowledge (justified belief) replaces former belief (belief that is no longer justified). In the past, however, we probably said, "I *know* "x." We revise how we speak of that previous "knowledge" in the light of new evidence.

Occasionally we say that we "don't know." If we really don't know, then we are frozen. We can't act. Knowledge enables action. Lack of knowledge hampers action. Usually, we wind up acting on our best belief of the moment. Life goes on, and we continue to collect justifications that a belief is true, i.e. that it constitutes knowledge. It is a spiral process.

So there has to be some sort of justification for a belief in order for it to be knowledge. But even more that that, the belief needs to be *true* to satisfy the middle part of the definition, justified true belief.

Saying that something is true has a kind of arrogance about it. But unless you believe something is true enough to act on it, then you really can't claim to be a (professional) knowledge worker. But believing something does not make it true. We all know that advertising is built on the premise that beliefs can often be formed without reference to the truth. Knowledge requires more than belief – truth . . . and evidence for the belief.

Knowledge, unlike information, is more than just an opinion – it is an opinion that a professional renders based on evidence. It is true. The mechanic who says, "This plane is ready to fly," knows what he or she is talking about. The artist who says, "you should use the blue color" is knowledgeable and knows more about colors than most of us. The farmer

---

Davenport and Prusak on Knowledge

"Knowledge is a fluid mix of framed experience, values, contextual information, and expert insight that provides a framework for evaluating and incorporating new experiences and information. It originates and is applied in the minds of knowers. In organizations, it often becomes embedded not only in documents and repositories, but also in organizational routines, processes, practices, and norms." Davenport, Homas H. and Prusak, Laurence, Working Knowledge. Boston: Harvard Business School. 1998. p. 5.

who can look at a herd and say, "That bull is better for breeding" knows something that others do not.

My knowledge is your information. Your knowledge is my information and we rely on each other's judgments to get our work done. Your information becomes my knowledge if, having examined it against my own experience, skills and knowledge, it "fits" into my body of knowledge and passes the truth test. What is true in your world may not be true in mine and different communities may come to different conclusions. But as communities overlap, their conclusions are called into question . . . and out of that interchange often comes new knowledge. Truth is not just a matter of opinion, but what is true may depend on our perspective, on where we are and how we see things – on what works in different situations.

As we live, we "know" some things to be true . . . because we act on them – and if they work, they are considered true. If my bridge stands, the information on which I based the design is now called knowledge (justified, true belief). If I jump out the window believing I can fly based on the "truth" of an LSD trip and die, in retrospect that is now "known" to have been just a belief and not "true" – not in conformity with reality.

Reality is a harsh judge of truth. Knowledge statements need to be true. What is truth and knowledge today may, in the course of events, turn out not to be true – in which case I will no longer know what I thought I knew. But making judgments about what is true and what is not true is at the heart of knowledge work. A true belief is the best judgment, based on evidence, which we make at a particular time.

So, the traditional definition of knowledge as "justified true belief" seems to serve us well and "truth" is without doubt the most important and most elusive part of our definition of knowledge.

Knowledge, Information and Data – some distinctions

Knowledge is often confused with information or even data. Information work and knowledge work are very different – and managing knowledge and managing information are different activities.

As we have pointed out, knowledge is *related* to data and information. Knowledge is the result of someone's (or a community's) judgments based on data and information.

Data, the set of discrete, objective facts about events in today's world often resides in computers, in databases and other electronic records. Information is data that has been given relevance and purpose

– contextualized perhaps, or sorted, evaluated, and "given shape" by what's included or what's excluded – a judgment has been applied to the data.

Knowledge is the justified true belief on which we base our judgments and actions. Making the judgments to manage information is one form of knowledge work.

Knowledge is not just intellectual in nature – it is the ability to do something of value – it is a competence that one has. In the work situation it is a competence to achieve the goals of an organization or task.

Knowledge is competence in doing work – a knowledgeable worker is a professional. We "know" what to do and doing what we know is our work. The work is taking information and data and "making" knowledge – a creative act to produce something of value that requires understanding.

> *"What we call knowledge, therefore, is not just a matter of local competence; it depends also on the orientation of these practices within broader constellations . . . Knowing in practice involves an interaction between the local and the global."*[32]

Knowledge work adds value, is done for a purpose, connects things, and puts them into a context. Knowledge Work is the creative "leap" that unites means and ends, tools and goals.

Wisdom – the Other Side of Knowledge

Wisdom is beyond knowledge. It is the "other side." Wisdom seldom comes with justification and goes beyond belief to a kind of certainty that comes not from criticism and examination but revelation – or long experience, testing beliefs by living, learning, observing and understanding how the world works.

That is why wisdom is often the purview of the enlightened and the religious – those who know and understand Truth and Justice and the Good. Wisdom speaks with capital letters. It is on a higher plain and relates to insights that reveal connections not readily grasped or understood, even by those who are very knowledgeable.

We can speak of knowledge workers, but it makes little sense to speak of wisdom workers. For you don't "make" wisdom. You have it and live it. Neither do you make wisdom for a living.

---

[32] Entienne Wenger. Communities of Practice. Learning, Meaning and Identity. Cambridge, 1998, p 141

Wise people are often, but not always, very knowledgeable. Some say that wisdom comes with age, but we all know that few are truly wise, regardless of the number of years on this earth. Wisdom is imbued with mystery and awe.

That is why hermeneutics, the art and science of understanding, is even more important in the realm of wisdom than knowledge. Beauty and truth are revealed and through the ages men and women have found sacred texts to be the "source" of wisdom and interpreting and understanding these texts is often the purview of a class of people who are not of this world.

Wisdom is, truly, "other worldly." It is not the purview of this book, nor is wisdom something that comes from accumulating knowledge, any more than knowledge comes from accumulating information.

We leave the world of wisdom to others. Understanding knowledge and the nature of knowledge work is a knotty enough task.

Inherently Democratic

Knowledge work is inherently democratic because it is done in and through communities of practice. We know this statement is not intuitively obvious to most people. I have written about democratic theory at another time and place.[33] I bring this matter up now to point out that the nature of knowledge work requires a situation in which communities are controlled by those who live and work in them. Knowledge work – and knowledge workers – will be most productive in democratic communities. Democracy is all about community life being controlled by those in the community.

Communities are democratic, although the organizations, societies and political structures associated with communities may not always be democratic. A democratic society is one in which there is an environment – a community – under the control of those who live and work in a community. Communities may also be oppressive and stifling and are often, at their core, conservative in character – for communities are the repositories of our common knowledge – our work culture.

Self-management and self-awareness are at the heart of professional work. All knowledge work requires self-management for it to be done the most efficiently, since it is a creative process. The self-management of knowledge work is done in and through communities of practice. The

---

[33] Megill, Kenneth, The New Democratic Theory, New York: Free Press (Macmillan). 1970.

knowledge worker, in order to do knowledge work, needs to be conscious (know) how other work fits into the work of the community and the employer. The knowledge worker, to use a military term, needs to know how a particular piece of work affects the "health of the fleet."[34]

If the Knowledge Age is to come to full flower, control will pass from the manager to the knowledge worker, not just because it is a better and more humane way to work, but because it is necessary for the work to get done efficiently.

Closed communities do something because it has always been done that way. The liberating aspect of democracy comes when it is open to other communities, to other cultures, and to new ways of living.

Not everyone agrees that knowledge work is inherently democratic. In fact, many business managers – who have an interest in preserving the control of the work place for managers – think of knowledge work as inherently colonial. This view is eloquently presented by Peter Drucker, in an article in Harvard Business Review ("The Coming New Organization") where he says that symphonies, hospitals and universities are the best example of knowledge work.

Drucker points to the British colonial administration in India as an excellent way to organize knowledge work. "The best example of a large and successful information-based organization and one without any middle management at all, is the British civil administration in India."[35] Drucker's comments show that there are no democratic tendencies at all in the view of knowledge management he adopts. He sees the elimination of middle management, with control remaining firmly in the hands of the colonial administration. It does capture rather vividly the view of a "well-run" organization taken by many management theorists. It is a colonial work place.

None of these work places, as described by Drucker, are organized democratically. He believes that they are the example of what he calls "the new organization" because they are based on control from above with a few people (director, professors, doctors) giving direction to large teams of people to perform the work. Middle managers are eliminated, he says, in these work environments.

He goes even further, however, by citing the British model for colonial rule as an excellent example of ruling without middle managers. A

---

[34] Thanks to Colonel (retired) Andy Nodine for this thought. See the appendix where more of Colonel Nodine's thoughts are presented.

[35] "The Coming New Organization, " Harvard Business Review on Knowledge Management, p. 8.

small number of colonial staff was able to control a large sub-continent for a time.

The colonial model is, indeed, the model of many who bring knowledge management into the work place. In the end, however, colonialism collapsed – in no small part due to the efforts of masses of people such as those led by Gandhi, who refused to cooperate with a colonial government. Colonialism is not a good model for knowledge work.

Learning, an essential part of a knowledge environment, is a voluntary activity – of a person understanding work and how that work fits into a community or communities.

Therefore, in the end, we must reject the colonial model and embrace the democratic model of community-based knowledge. Knowledge work is done in and through communities and to be most effective and efficient, they are democratic. The colonial model will not work – not for long and not now.

Leadership is based on very different social norms and assumptions than management. It begins with a focus on and enhancement of the value of work.

Work and Activity

Developing a new work culture more suited to knowledge work begins with the recognition that there is a fundamental difference between activity and work.[36]

Work requires effort/activity, but unless something happens and something of value is produced, no work is done. In order to do knowledge work, we need to get real answers to real questions. One engineer demonstrates this principle by going to a wall and pushing against it. He says "I can push on this wall all day long, do it with skill, put in great effort, follow directions, be creative in how I push . . . . but unless the wall moves, no work is done." Of course, this assumes that the work is to move the wall. If the purpose of the work is to test the wall to see if it will stand pressure, then pushing on the wall would indeed be work, for it achieves a goal.

---

[36] As one observer of business life summed it up: "Haw began to realize the difference between activity and production." Spencer Johnson, Who Moved my Cheese? An Amazing Way to Deal with Change in Your Work and Your Life. New York: Putnam, 1998, p. 42. The cheese book captures in a very succinct way the transformation of work from merely being present to making something happen.

Knowledge work involves action – activity – but it is a particular kind of activity – one of work – of movement. Something happens when you do knowledge work. You are engaged. The world is changed. Work involves accomplishing something. We learned the formula: Work = Force times Distance (w=f x d) in high school physics. Work is that part of what we *do* (doing is the "F" in the equation) that moves us toward our goal (our mission, our vision is the "D" in the equation). Work adds value to an activity – something *happens*.

Knowledge is sometimes contrasted with action. "Those who can't do, think." Actually, with our definition, knowledge is work; knowing is a particular kind of action – it involves work (W(work)=F(force) X D(distance) – moving objects (ideas) from place to place in order to do something – to answer questions like "Is it a good idea to . . . ." To make something of value.

The knowledge worker provides results – the products of thinking. Knowledge work is more than just being at work. It is making something of value to others.

Making knowledge is a purposeful activity that sorts through what information is relevant and useful. Knowledge workers then combine that information into new products, new ideas, and new decisions that are of value.

An Answer to a Question

A simple and refined description of the knowledge making process is: Knowledge is the answer to a question such as: "Is it a good idea to . . . ?" Making choices and judgments is at the heart of making knowledge. In order for the answer to be knowledge, it needs to be a justified true belief. The product of a knowledge worker is a set of judgments . . . of beliefs that are supportable by evidence that the (professional) knowledge worker believes (for good reason) are true.

The process of knowledge identification also includes defining and identifying the "customers" of that knowledge . . . those who need it as information to do their business.

As we have said before, making knowledge is an act of combining, synthesizing and integrating. It involves selecting, pulling out, noting similarities and differences. Knowing involves discarding – and assembling. Above all, knowledge work is work of ordering and putting things together . . . . integrating. The process of integrating is more than simply gathering together . . . it requires the creation of a new product that is different from any of the parts that go into its making. Integration – taking information from different sources, applying skill, learning and judgment to the information is how knowledge is made.

Later we shall describe the essence of the knowledge-making process is what software developers call the spiral methodology:

- Plan a little
- Build a little
- Deploy a little

We would add: Learn a lot.

This process – thinking spirally – is at the heart of knowledge work, for it is the result of doing something by applying the force (F) of our collective information and experience to the question that helps us reach our goal (D), "Is it a good idea to . . . ?" How far we move the wall toward an answer to that question tells us the amount of work done in that day. Knowledge work is the work of producing new ideas, solutions, and ways of thinking about problems – old and new. Knowledge work involves solving problems and completing projects.

It is more than simply gathering information (although that may be a step in making knowledge). It requires creating a product – a judgment that is an answer to a question. Something happens. Judgments that others can rely upon are made.

Going to Work

The distinction between "free" and "work" time is at the heart of what we call the industrial mode of production. That is replaced in the knowledge age by a professional attitude toward work. For many of us work connotes doing stuff we really don't want to do. In other words, we have to work so we can have "free" time. Work time is the time someone else organizes and controls. Free time is ours. The separation of work time from free time is one of the defining characteristics of the industrial work culture.

This act of "going to work" is the essence of the industrial mode of production:

- work is separate from leisure
- there is "work time" and "free time"
- you are paid for your "work time"

> **The Right to Be Lazy**
> In the late nineteenth century, Paul Lafarge (Karl Marx's son-in-law) published a little book called, The Right to Be Lazy. The book, originally written in French, has recently been translated and re-published by Fifth Season Press (Ardomore, Pa), 1999. Lafarge contrasts the "right to work" to the "right to be lazy" – a right never recognized by any society that we know of. Perhaps as the Knowledge Age matures, the importance of the right to be lazy will be recognized.

* you are "on the clock"
* you are "at your desk"
* you are "on the line"
* you "do your job"
* management coordinates
* owners make decisions
* work is divided up and parceled out.
* work is routine/mundane
* work takes place in a space at a specific time

Our work culture is built around these basic characteristics. Work starts and stops when you are "on the clock." While working on the clock, your time belongs to your employer, who organizes, directs and manages your work time.

John Jerome, an acute observer of human behavior, picks up the distinction between work and mere effort. If the wall moves, it is work . . . if it does not, it is just effort, without work. He contrasts this with the definition of work he was brought up with . . . work is to be avoided or gotten out of.

Work is what fulfills us. It is what makes us whole. He also captures the essence of the attitude toward work that is needed to best do knowledge work. "Movement in response to force is work." Work results in an actual product. Rather than learning to get out of work, the knowledge worker embraces work, becomes involved in it and works collaboratively with others to answer interesting questions. Although such an attitude may seem idealistic, anyone who has been involved in truly creative work knows that work can be amongst the most exciting and invigorating activities of life.

Work is What Fulfills Us

"Anthropologist Turnbull's[37] fantasy about work as whatever one happens to be doing at the time seems worth trying to achieve. There is another sense of the word that is similarly cheerful. Work, says the dictionary, is the transference of energy produced by the motion of the point of application of a force. I can't quite get my mind around that – the language ought to be able to do better with such a subject – but I think I get the idea. Push on something – or pull – and it moves, that was work. If it doesn't budge, it was merely effort.

"In this sense – call it Turnbullian – lifting a champagne glass to your lips is work. So is stepping into a hot bath. Movement in response to force is work. Add time to the measurement and the result is "power." These quantifications are in no way moral.

"I find such definitions deeply comforting. Somehow in my bringing up I was taught quite another definition: work was to be got out of. Work was our punishment for being born, being alive and only suckers even attempted to expiate that sin. Work was to be kept to a minimum, done as little as possible, dodged, shifted off onto others. And, if all else failed, done in the quickest, easiest, least energy taxing way possible."

---

[37] Colin Turnbull (1924–1994), was born in England and died in the United States. He wrote several anthropological studies of people in Africa, Tibet and Canada. See http://www.colinturnbull.com/author.html for more information on Turnbull.

"It wasn't entirely my parents who were responsible for this perversion. They set chores and expected them to be accomplished, but that was work as duty, not punishment. Perhaps it was the school system, which persisted in laying on empty drills and exercises long after we'd gotten the concept, when the willing part of our attention had gone on to other matters. Teachers demanded the copying down of things, the making of lists, and the filling of pages. It was the same in anything else that adults organized for kids. It was not a scam we could ever have articulated, but we recognized it clearly enough, in our not-so-innocent little hearts; they were keeping us busy. If left to our own devices, whatever we would busy ourselves with would obviously be wasteful, destructive, violent, or sinful. We were being kept in line.[38]

"On the other hand, work was, always, to be taken full credit for. Verisimilitude – the appearance of working – was therefore desirable. I can still remember the embarrassment I felt at seeing workers spring to their feet and try to appear busy when the boss showed up. Furthermore, work's result in actual product – acres plowed, bushels harvested, cords stacked – was the ultimate value, worth far more than the money it might bring. I suppose my attitude toward wealth got twisted at the same time as it did toward work."[39]

---

[38] Tom Sawyer understood all of this very well.

[39] John Jerome, On Turning Sixty-Five. Notes from the Field. New York: Random House, 2000, pp. 141–143.

Playing Office is not Work

The organization of work in a serial, hierarchical system is done at the top by managers who coordinate the individual work of individual workers. The industrial assembly line is the model – whether on the shop floor or in offices. Complex management systems are developed, tested, and implemented to bring the work together, to wring out inefficiencies and to see that work is done in the shortest time at the lowest possible cost. Analyses of work processes show that only about twenty to thirty percent of the time spent "at work" is spent actually doing work.[40] The percentage is not as important as the realization that when we are "at" work, much of the time we do not "do" work.

This is not because we are "bad" employees, but because our work environment and resulting culture is organized in such a way that it fosters "putting in time" over productive labor – even in the most productive organizations.

Playing office is not work. Anyone who has spent even a little bit of time in an office knows that much of that time is spent in activities relating to the office, not to the work being done. Much of the time "at work" is spent waiting for someone to decide what needs to be done or for someone else to complete work that must be done before the "real" work can start. Workflow analysis and business reengineering focuses on wringing these inefficient moments out of the system, but the problem is endemic in a work culture that is built around work being done in one place with free time being spent somewhere else.

Travel is not work (unless you are the pilot or part of the crew that gets us there). Travel is, indeed, often necessary, but that does not make it work. Travel, like meetings, is often a substitute for work. As one astute observer noted, "I don't know how often I have stopped working to go to a meeting or travel somewhere."[41]

When we divorce work from showing up for work, we begin to look at the world in a way that is fitting for the creation of knowledge in the digital age and a different kind of work culture develops. And it makes sense.

Today's work environments are not geared towards supporting knowledge work. The nature of the work itself is changing faster than our work culture. The work requires a different type of culture to use available technology to its fullest potential.

---

[40] This figure comes from Herb Schantz.
[41] Colonel Terry Balven, USAF, the military leader of the Integrated Digital Environment Project. See the appendix for his description of the project.

The Magic of Understanding

When we are knowledge workers, what we do is understand information. A bit later, we shall look at hermeneutics as the science/art of understanding. For now let us notice that we see information as part of a context . . . a context that enables us to answer questions and solve problems. The "production" of knowledge is a process of understanding. We bring our life, experience, expertise, and skills base to our work. And we bring previous understandings/knowledge with us.

Based on what we know and information which we gain from others, the knowledge worker makes informed judgments about "Is it a good idea to?" This decision then becomes part of the knowledge store of the community.

When that knowledge is transmitted to someone else, that person puts it through a filter of life, experience, expertise, and skill's base as part of the information used for another person to make judgments in a different field all together. This understanding is the magic that transforms the world in which we live . . . and the magic that makes us human.

> **The Ontology of Work**
> Perhaps the only philosophical work devoted specifically to the nature of work was done by Georg Lukacs (1885–1971), a German-trained Hungarian philosopher. Lukacs is best know for his seminal works on aesthetics. In a late work called the "ontology of work", he said: "Work can be seen as the fundamental phenomenon – model of social being (Seins). Georg Lukacs, Ontology of Work, p. 9 "Work is, in its essence – Wechselbeziehung (exchange relationship) between nature and man (society)" (p. 8) and "Work – uninterrupted production of the New" (p. 26). Lukacs understood that work is the fundamental activity of man (men and women) that makes us what we are. The creative act results from working with nature, the environment, or others to make something new.

But then it is not so magical at all . . . it is just doing what we do when we make knowledge. We do that by:

- Identifying the problem. Knowing what question is being answered is normally half the task – or more.
- Accumulating. Gathering the information, the right information, recalling the right information – and just the right information – to answer

> **The Art of Choosing What to Know**
> "Words like 'understanding' require some caution because they can easily reflect an implicit assumption that there is some universal standard of the knowable. In the abstract, anything can be known, and the rest is ignorance. But in a complex world in which we must find a livable identity, ignorance is never simply ignorance, and knowing is not just a matter of information. In practice, understanding is always straddling the known and unknown in a subtle dance of the self. It is a delicate balance. Wherever we are, understanding in practice is the art of choosing what to know and what to ignore in order to proceed with our lives."[42]

the question. The criterion for what information is "right" depends on the circumstances, context, and needs of the knowledge worker.

- Discarding. Normally more information is accumulated than is used . . . for the creative process of making knowledge is one of identifying and shaping. Identifying what is relevant and what is not is as important as accumulating information. "Precision" in information retrieval is one way to refer to this process. But what "precisely" is useful often requires going back to the source, or a different source . . . for it is an iterative spiral process.
- Comparing. Much of knowledge work is identifying what is similar and what is not similar – what something is "like" or "not like."
- Hypothesizing – drawing a conclusion – one that is not certain – is tentative. The hypothesis may be with the knowledge person all along the process (it is a spiral after all).
- Concluding. At some point a decision is made . . . "this is the right answer" – I know the answer to this question. A conclusion may come right away – or it may be at the conclusion of a long and involved process. The quality of the judgment, not the time it takes to make the judgment is the essential element. Knowledge requires certainty . . . not the kind of certainty that comes from faith, revelation or perception, but the certainty that this is the best answer to a properly formed question. The conclusion requires a reference to the body of knowledge of the community. How does it "fit" with the conclusions that others have made?
- Disseminating. Making the conclusions known and available to others who need it to do their knowledge work.

---

[42] Etienne Wenger, Communities of Practice. Learning, Meaning and Identify. Cambridge: Cambridge University Press, 1998, 41.

- Evaluating. Out of the work process, new issues arise that may need an answer. Depending on the nature of the work, the problems to be solved may come from the discovery/work process itself. In other cases, work comes from others . . . both within and without the community. Part of the evaluation process involves adjusting the body of knowledge, identifying that what we "used to know" is no longer knowledge and what is "new" knowledge. Knowledge work is spiral.

People describe the process of understanding in many different ways. It is the basic process of creation . . . of work in an environment where knowledge is made. Similar descriptions, sometimes with more or less steps, are found in many places, such as:

- The scientific process. Sometimes this is called the "scientific method" – the way that scientific work is done.
- The creative process. An artist generally describes a similar process.
- Life-cycle management. Information management speaks of managing information from "birth to destruction" – often with different ways to describe the process depending on the perspective of the viewer.

In the process of doing knowledge work, many communities may be touched, some more than others. In fact, some say that the most creative part of work often comes where communities overlap . . . and what is taken as "common sense" in one community is seen as a new and exciting way of looking at the world and work by another community.

Creativity

The process of creativity, which sometimes, but not always, involves serendipity, is often called a "gift." We know that some people possess more creativity than others and none of us can be creative in all that we do. Some people are better mechanics than others . . . or better gardeners . . . or better story tellers. People can learn how to be creative – sometimes through an apprentice relationship with a master. An apprentice does not just do what the master does – but learns "peripherally" by circling around and absorbing the values of the master. How learning takes place in an environment where knowledge work is the norm is no longer a mystery. Much has been written and spoken about a "learning organization" as one in which learning becomes imbued into the very work of the business.

Others learn through meditation, observation, critical self-examination, play or other means. Creativity is at the heart of knowledge work – and at the heart of what it means to be human. Creativity comes within and from a community. When we make knowledge we make something new.

"Making something new" becomes a value in the knowledge age. Coloring outside the lines – seeing things differently – are positive traits for the knowledge worker – traits that would impede an industrial production line.

The Interconnectivity of Knowledge

The terms knowledge management and knowledge workers are now part of our vocabulary – and no doubt are here to stay. Like all new terms that enter into our daily language, they take on many meanings as people become used to the notion that one kind of work is knowledge work. It is the work of coming to justified, true, beliefs.

Knowledge is developed and grows within a community. Knowledge also changes as a community of practice develops new knowledge. This interconnectivity underscores the importance of information sharing to enable good knowledge work. If one person's knowledge is another person's information and that person relies on that knowledge as evidence for his or her knowledge work, then ways need to be in place for that person to know if/when the first person changes his or her mind because of new evidence.

Within a scientific community the interconnectivity of knowledge is embodied in the knowledge store of the community. Managing knowledge stores and is an essential part of knowledge managing and marshaling.

Work (and life) is never certain. But we can know, within a community, enough to do our work. Knowledge work is linked intricately with another concept – that of community of practice.

Knowledge work is enhanced by working in and through communities of practice in an integrated digital environment.

Knowledge Management

Knowledge Management is the discipline of making relevant knowledge available as information so that users can make timely, valid decisions that increase the productivity of their work.

Much of the discussion among those who talk about knowledge management fails to make the distinction between knowledge and information management rigorously enough and leads to great confusion. Clarity and agreement on definitions are necessary in order to progress to be made. Knowledge management needs to be seen as a fundamentally different process than information management – it cannot just re-name an old process.

A healthy community of practice enhances the process of knowledge creation and management. It evaluates and validates the work of the members of the community and builds a body of knowledge. Knowledge is organic – and like all things organic – it decays if it is not used. Knowledge is not "used up" when it is used – it, in fact, grows in value and use to the members of community. The process of encouraging knowledge creation and impeding decay of knowledge over time, validating knowledge and removing useless knowledge are important tasks of knowledge management.

If knowledge is "justified true belief," then the term "knowledge management" does not make a lot of sense. How can we "manage" beliefs? We cannot – at least in the traditional sense of managing as direction.

What we can do is manage a knowledge store, make it accessible, organize it and do all of the other activities that go into information management. But we manage it as information, for one person's knowledge is another person's information. We can also encourage knowledge production. As what people know grows – and sometimes changes, the knowledge store reflects those changes. A knowledge store is not a permanent, fixed encyclopedia of knowledge, but an organic creation of a community of practice.

The term "knowledge management," however, is often used simply as another name for information management – with a special focus on "tacit" information that may or may not be made explicit and accessible to an organization. It needs to mean more than that.

We manage information as information – we organize it, index it, put it in context, preserve it, retrieve it and throw it away – all of the things that we do with information. But managing knowledge differs fundamentally from managing information. It is about providing an environment, nurturing a community, with supporting technology so that judgments can be made – the work of knowledge workers.

Because information is someone else's knowledge, the information value may be more reliable. This makes it more useful to others. One justification for holding a belief is that someone else, who is respected, believes it is a justified true belief (knowledge). We often rely on others for our knowledge as we work together in a community of practice.

Knowledge management is about improving the effectiveness and value of knowledge work. As we change work processes – how work is done – the work needs to be done more effectively – as measured by the ability to meet the needs of those who use the products of knowledge work. "Effectiveness" speaks to the value of the work of the organization to satisfy the needs of the organization's customer(s). **Knowledge management is about improving the effectiveness and value of knowledge work.**

One kind of knowledge worker assumes the responsibility to "manage" the knowledge of an organization or community. The knowledge manager serves as a knowledge consultant to insure that the essential information of a business is preserved and accessible to all who have a need for it.

In an environment where knowledge is created, there is a role for a knowledge manager with specific tasks that may go beyond those of information managers. The knowledge manager:

- Enables access to information needed to do work.[43]
- Ensures that access replaces reporting.
- Ensures that the owner of information is responsible for its integrity, accuracy, and timeliness.[44]
- Encourages owners of information to share, rather than hoard, their information.
- Determines who needs information to do their work and helps them get it.[45] In an integrated digital environment, the application (the set of business processes often automated using software) and the knowledge worker determine what information is needed.
- Provides capabilities and technologies to allow the owners of information to make it accessible
- Determines whether the work of the organization is done more productively and effectively, not just whether the parts of work are done efficiently.

---

[43] In the pre-digital (paper) environment the information manager collects, organizes, stores, and retrieves information. Managing information, in a pre-digital environment is primarily about how to move and store information. In a paper environment information managers function as information gatekeepers, because they are the ones who know where the files or information are located.

[44] In a pre-digital (paper) environment, information was gathered into collections (record collections, libraries, databases, etc) with custodians in charge of the collections.

[45] In a pre-digital (paper) environment, position determined who controlled work. In an organization based on division of labor, information needs are limited because your job was limited. In a digital environment, work can be done collaboratively in projects and information needs increase as the number of roles played increase.

Knowledge Marshaling

Knowledge marshaling is akin to knowledge management with the added dimension of organizing knowledge for a purpose or aim.

Creating a knowledge marshalling capability is essential to transform its work culture so that it can take full advantage of the benefits of technology.

Because of the reigning confusion about what is knowledge management what is information management, it might be better to use the term knowledge marshalling, even though it has a kind of military tone to it.

This knowledge marshalling capability needs to become ubiquitous in an organization. It requires leadership and example at the highest levels to build this new capability.

Roc Myers[46] suggests a term, "knowledge marshalling" that might be a preferable, if not yet a standard, term:

It is something like knowledge management, but may be a better because:

- Marshaling means gathering pieces together for a purpose.
- Marshaling (unlike management) focuses on the use of knowledge, not its content or structure.
- Marshaling seems a more useful term because it better describes what should be done with knowledge than "management."

From an organizational perspective, there appears to be a continued merging of knowledge management into the regular and orderly patterns of organizational operations. The notion that knowledge both in information systems and in employee's heads needs to be managed and leveraged has taken root in most organizations. Knowledge management initiatives are being funded both as individual change initiatives and as part of a larger information and organizational restructuring.

As we shall see communities of practice are no longer geographically limited because of the new technologies that enable us to do collaborative work. Although there are an increasing number of digital tools that enable information sharing and collaborative work, work processes are still often serial in nature.

In order to grow and prosper, communities of practice which create knowledge work need an integrated digital environment, an environment in which information is shared, not hoarded. This environment requires

---

[46] http://www.pirp.harvard.edu/pubs_pdf/myers/Myers_StratKnowledgecr_P004.pdf

technologies, and we shall look at some of them in the next chapter. However, even if we have the potential to get the best available information to all that need it, we still spend countless hours developing detailed periodic reports. Often those creating the reports receive little or no benefit from them. We develop numerous copies of the same information, yet there can be as many versions of the information as there are copies since each person may add individual comments, marginal notes, etc. Training, which can be embedded in the work process itself is still both independent of the job and is usually separate from the organization's knowledge stores. While most see these problems as tool related, we contend that these are fundamental problems embedded in the work culture. We are still working in an industrial culture where the assumption is that there is an assembly line, work is done in small pieces, by interchangeable workers, serially. The work is managed by a foreman/manager and passed up the line for someone else's addition. The end product is not seen, known or understood by each piece-worker.

The monumental changes that could be enacted by existing technology (often only cubicles away) lie dormant, un-enacted because co-workers are often clueless as to what others are doing, how they are doing it, and how the work they are doing affects the overall health of the organization. If their information were pooled, their efforts aggregated, their solutions shared, their collaboration encouraged and rewarded, their culture will change in such a way that the work itself will be transformed.

CHAPTER 5

Integrated Digital Environment

We come now to the second of the "new" concepts that enable us to understand the transformation of work in the knowledge age. Like "knowledge work" and "community of practice," the term "integrated digital environment" unites concepts that do not, intuitively at least, seem to belong together.

An integrated digital environment is one in which there is immediate access to information needed to do work.

While automation in general and an integrated digital environment in specific are critical to the knowledge worker in the Age of Knowledge, effective automation is about more than wires and computers . . . it is about how we do work. An integrated digital environment is about real people doing real work. An integrated digital environment is exactly that, an environment. It describes the atmosphere, the conditions, the culture, and the "stuff" that makes possible a new way of working – working as knowledge creators. The adjectives that describe that environment, "integrated" and "digital" mean that there are wires and computers, that's the digital part. Integrated describes the ubiquitous connectivity that allows the worker access to all the information needed in order to do real work.

The term "integrated digital environment" is not as widely used as "knowledge work" and "community of practice" in knowledge management discussions. But it is part of the language of information technology. In the IT world, IDE is the term used to describe the technological (generally understood as the hardware, software and connectivity tools) of an organization or an enterprise.

Depending on the focus, each of the terms "Integrated." "digital," and "environment" can become the most important.

- "Digital" refers to the technology that enables knowledge work. It is about the wires and computers that are the tools of the knowledge trade. It includes the connectivity that enables collaborative work to be done.
- "Environment" refers to the surroundings, to all of the background that makes knowledge work viable. The terms "digital" and "integrated" both modify "environment." A digital environment is contrasted with an analog environment. A digital environment is the world of computers and people who are connected together as a community does its work.
- The "integration" of a digital environment comes through web technology – through linking together communities of practice and disparate individuals and groups within an organization. The web came possible when people adopted protocols – standards – for communication. These standards create an environment in which information sharing is the norm. A new world of discourse arose.

The initials IDE were initially used to refer to "integrated data environment" – a technical environment in which databases could be integrated, generally by intermediate data bases (or middle ware) that enables databases created for disparate situations to be accessible from a single source.

The integration in a digital environment increases the possibility for knowledge work to become the norm, not the exception. Through the adoption and use of communication standards, open architectures, increased communication capabilities and agreements to share appropriate information among business units and throughout industries a new environment necessary for knowledge work is created. This environment includes technologies, but more importantly, it includes ways of working that emphasize and enable information sharing.

The term integrated digital environment in the United States government was popularized by former Vice-President Albert Gore as a part of the reinvention of government movement to refer to the technical environment necessary for a new way to do government business.

The Department of Defense has had a formally constituted program for several years to develop an integrated digital environment and the term is widely used. Each of the Services, as is normally the case, uses the term in different ways and there is no agreement on what the term means.[47]

For some, an integrated digital environment is identical with an integrated data environment – an environment in which data can be shared among various agencies, among contractors and the government, and among businesses within an industry. In the industrial world it often refers to ways in which different businesses, both within the same company and among various companies, can share data and information using a common language or database.

For others, however, the phrase takes on a more robust meaning. In the US Air Force the focus in the integrated digital environment project quickly moved beyond developing wires and computers to a new way of doing business. In this chapter we shall use the term "integrated digital environment" to mean an environment in which the information needed to do business is immediately accessible. This is the definition adopted by the Air Force project and being used by a Work Culture Transformation Board established to implement the conclusions of that project.

Principles of an Integrated Digital Environment

The age of knowledge work is being shaped and propelled by technological developments. Not that the machine is driving the new ways of thinking about work, but enabling new ways to work. These new ways to work do not require bringing workers together in an industrial setting and open up new opportunities for a more humane and efficient way to do work. Communities can be digital, not just spatial. Time and space are transformed when we enter together into the digital environment to do our work.

In a good working environment, those who need information and know who the owner is can access that information without requiring special formatting, copies, packing, and sending.

The two principles of the owner/creator as the keeper of information and replacing reporting with access underlie the proper use of technology. They are, in a sense, a mirror image of each other. In order to replace reporting with access, it is necessary to identify the "owner" of information. This is not a trivial process and is the essence of steps II and III in the methodology presented in the next section.

---

[47] See the appendix for a description of the Air Force project.

The Principles of an Integrated Digital Environment

1. The owner/creator of information/data is the keeper and is responsible for its accuracy and timeliness.
2. Access to information replaces reporting.
3. Corporate memory (the essential evidence of an organization) is retained and is accessible in the "Knowledge Store" for reuse.

These principles can be articulated and arranged in various ways, but they accurately describe the integrated digital environment in which knowledge work can best be done.

Reporting requirements can be reduced or eliminated as the same or better information is accessible once work is done in a web based environment. This single step creates immediate incentives to move to the web-based environment because it reduces some of the most onerous work of an organization.

These principles – identifying the owner of information and making the work of the owner accessible to those who need it to do their work – require the adoption of the values of trust and sharing that are the key to the transformation of the work process. These values are realizable because the technology enables us to open up our workspaces so that others can "look over our shoulder as we work." One, specific, way this can be done is to adopt the second principle of an integrated digital environment – "Replace reporting with access."

If work is done in a collaborative web environment, it is possible for one person to view the work of another, even as it is being done. This enables authorized persons to have immediate access to the most recent owner-maintained and, therefore most accurate information without doing a query and without bothering the person doing the work.

The key, of course, is the ability for people to authorize access in order to be assured that the access is not abused. Properly done, this capability implements a trusting relationship – where trust is understood as being assured that the information that I have access to is the most up to date – and the best available judgment of another person.

Once the values that underlie an integrated digital environment are put into practice and work is done in an information-sharing environment, access to information replaces reporting. The reporting function is characteristic of hierarchical work environments where much time that could be productively used is taken up reporting from one level of the organization to another.

Collaboration has two time components. In the short-term view, collaboration implies more than one person working in unison on developing a knowledge product. The long-term view of collaboration concerns the organization's ability to leverage and maximize ideas and work products to produce future work products, i.e., a present-day worker is collaborating with one who has gone before by re-using the ideas, work, knowledge of the past. When an organization has whole-heartedly adopted collaboration concepts, its ability to innovate, create and reuse existing information rises dramatically.

Working collaboratively on line

In a digital environment, much collaborative work is done online and members of the work community may be dispersed around the world. The challenge in making the transition in the work culture to embrace online collaborative work involves both a comfort with and understanding of how to work together. The social factors, including trust, focused goals and clear responsibilities, must be in place for a functioning online work team.

A properly developed collaborative environment enables greater, not less, personal interaction among participants. Much time in meetings is spent exchanging information and doing household chores that can be done more efficiently using a collaborative online environment.

In collaborative environments, meetings are places for personal interaction, no receiving information. When a community comes together, discussion is encouraged, for discussion is often best done in person. The function of meetings shifts from giving reports to sharing knowledge and establishing working relationships. Collaboration replaces a serial, step-by-step work process with one in which work is done simultaneously by a number of different communities. The communities are linked, when and where appropriate, into networks. Work is becoming network centric, not system centric. The term and concept of network is imbedded in the term "internet."

In a collaborative environment, information is contained in a network of knowledge stores that are related to one another in a set of business processes . . . an application. These business processes, however, do not stand alone, but get meaning from other related applications. The same principles apply to bodies of knowledge of a community of practice. Collaboration is the way work is done in a network-centric environment.

The Power of Working in a Web Environment[48]

The single, most important development in information management technology for knowledge management is the development of web technology. Web technology encompasses both Internets and Intranets and gives us the ability to store information close to the site where it is created and used and yet be accessible to anyone with proper authorization on the net.

   The current and developing technologies that enable knowledge work to be done are those used to create and enhance the web environment. The Internet is a network of networks and a set of standards that enables networks to talk with one another. A web environment enables work to be done differently from the industrial mode of production, whether the work is done on an intranet, on the internet or as part of collaborative tools.

1. Web technology allows us to point to information, rather than copy it.

Whenever we copy information, we assume an obligation for its maintenance. By transmitting this information to others, we are responsible for its authenticity. We assume some degree of stewardship. Web technology allows us to "look over the shoulder" of the creator/owner of the information and to get the "most right" version of the information/data at any given time from the source authority. Web-based forms can collect information. Information needs to be collected only once – and used many times by different uses for very different purposes. Much information required by forms can be collected from user profiles and does not require repeated re-entry. The technology allows us very easily to create, publish, update, modify, and maintain information and data. It enables reporting to be replaced by access to information.

2. Web technology frees us from the traditional publishing cycle.

We no longer need to wait for the monthly deadline before information can be disseminated to the intended audience. If we have new information that we have discovered, created, assembled, or developed, we can

---

[48] The author is indebted to Harry Pape, Col USAF (ret), who helped him understand the power of working in a web environment.

make it accessible immediately without intermediaries. The technology allows us to attach meta-data (information about the information) that enables us to identify information about the document or item, such as which version it is. Web technology enables us to collect, retain and make available corporate memory. Web technology allows us to look over the shoulder of a colleague without disturbing them. It also enables us to easily emulate successful presentations of information by copying information and/or ways of presentation. Etiquette dictates recognizing the source, but the practice of copying quickly becomes ubiquitous in a web environment. As one keeper of the corporate memory in an organization said, "I have been around long enough, so I can copy." This is an important attitude that is shared in successful learning organizations. Having your information or your way of presenting information copied is a compliment of the highest order. It is flattering for others to rely on you or your information, particularly if they are courteous in attributing their source.

3. The technology allows us to interact with our peers, our customers, and our audience.

Publishing on the web is not a one-way broadcast of information. It provides for the ability to dialogue with the reader, to get instant feedback by way of acknowledgment or comment, and, more importantly, for interaction with the customer that enhances the value of the communication transaction and can customize the information needed by a particular customer. For example, when staff interacts with customers in a web environment they are able to tailor an offering to be most useful to the particular customer. A customer does not need to know about the parts of the information that won't fit their needs, so these parts need not appear. Web-based information systems are not flat, two-dimensional databases. They are rich, drillable collections of information. Web technology encourages collaboration as a way of working.

Access to information in the web environment is controlled so only those who need it can have access to what they need. Confidentially and security are protected at least as well, or better, than in the paper world. Information available on the web is safeguarded so that the creator's ownership of it is assured. It opens up new ways for owners/creators to make their knowledge accessible without preparing a report or publishing it.

As we begin to develop a collaborative way of working, we also begin to make new demands on others. We expect them to make the products of their work that we need accessible to us. We begin to make demands on others not by forcing others, but by offering to take what they make, value it and use it in our work.

This requires developing relationships with those who have that information. It also requires leadership willing to remove obstacles, support workers with enabling technology, and reward sharing and collaboration.

It Takes Toys to Play in Today's Sandbox

The tools developed within the web environment enable and foster the cultural transformation.

The various forms of "new mail," both voice -mail and e-mail lead to great changes in organizational interaction. Various forms of synchronous and asynchronous discussion tools enable real changes in organizational culture and learning. Autonomous agents that do everything from remind us of meetings and tasks to executing stock trades. Instant notifications based on parameters set by the organization are becoming a routine part of our lives. Telecommunication tools such as cell phones and various assistants, along with portable lap-top computers, make the office mobile.

The introduction of e-mail enables people to communicate quickly with one another. It also enables people to circumvent the established hierarchies – and it eliminates space (and sometimes time) as a limiting factor in organizing work. E-mail revolutionizes communication in organizational life, but it is modeled on paper-based culture and brings a number of pathologies. E-mail replaces many personal communications that should remain personal. Many people manage all their files through enormous e-mail in-boxes. The same files may be captured and stored in multiple versions. Discerning the right one to send is sometimes difficult. E-mail is still mail, though it can be more insidious – the work done in e-mail is the same as writing on a piece of paper, going to a copying machine and sending copies. It is just faster, but not smarter, and enables copies to be sent even more easily than using a copy machine to make paper copies.

Instant messaging and its various forms of "chatting" in real time encourage and enable collaboration on knowledge work. It is possible to carry on several conversations at once, with a changing cast of characters. Many different peer-to-peer connectivity tools are being deployed. They are used for wide range of activities, from sharing music and movie files to enabling project managers to effectively manage projects independent of time and space concerns.

Document sharing is another tool that promotes collaboration. One person can write a document, put it in an accessible place, a group (one selected for the purpose or an "open" group) can work on that document – i.e. see what the document is, make changes that are highlighted for all to see, comment, etc. etc. What used to take a meeting can now be done using collaborative tools.

Electronic mail, instant messaging and document sharing do not give us a new culture, but they free us to think about a new relationship to information – a relationship based on sharing and getting the information one worker needs by looking over the shoulder of the owner/creator of that information.

The tools evolving in the web technology open a much greater opportunity (one that is just beginning to be explored) to interact with and use the information of those who have gone before us. The corporate memory of an organization is now recognized as one of its most valuable assets. Knowledge management tools capture tacit knowledge and make it explicit. Records management systems enable us to capture and access records within our environment.

Search and retrieval tools combine with descriptions of meta-data to open access to the knowledge of others.

Developing the infrastructure of the public utilities for the new work culture is one supporting condition for developing a new work culture.

The development of these technologies provides the possibility for developing a new kind of environment for work. This environment can be both digital and integrated.

Transforming a work process means making the information needed to do that work accessible and making the products of that work (knowledge) available as information to others. Transforming the work culture goes beyond improving business processes. It requires understanding the work of the enterprise, its communities and the domains of the communities.

It also requires a technical infrastructure that makes connectivity ubiquitous. Digital connectivity needs to be as dependable and as widespread as access to water and electricity. Connectivity is the "public utility" of the integrated digital environment. This infrastructure, combined with work culture transformation, enables the benefits of technology to be realized.

Working in a Digital Environment

As we noted before, work is done in a place, but that place no longer needs to be a shared physical location. As knowledge workers do more and more work, the environment is characterized by a set of overlapping communities. Work is done "in" an environment. The environment includes both the physical (wires, computers, buildings, etc.) attributes and the social relationships (friends, neighbors, co-workers, professional colleagues, etc.). It includes the physical infrastructure, the "public utilities" that enable work to be done. It also includes the social infrastructure, a group of good friends, chat groups, colleagues, supporters and critics alike.

Creating an environment in which information is shared is an important part of the culture transformation – and one that will not always be simple to create. Sharing is not not a nice thing in the knowledge age. It is a necessity for work to be done efficiently and effectively.

In a paper-based, non-digital, environment, the work was determined by who "owned" or "held" the paper at a particular point in time. Work flowed from place-to-place and each person contributed the amount of work necessary and appropriate to move the paper on to the next place.

In the paper world, decisions were made by moving documents up and down chains. This decision-making procedure is required by the technology of paper – there is basically one authoritative copy of what is being considered and one person can look at it at a time.

When information or knowledge is the product worked with and paper is the medium for capturing and transmitting that knowledge, even if multiple copies of a document are made (distributed), only one person can look at a one copy at a time. Even if two or three are gathered together and looking at the same copy, the work process is essentially individualized. And once someone makes notes on a copy, a new record is created.

When one person is "finished," the document passes to the next persons. Records (the document that passes from one person to another) arise in the course of doing business. Decisions are made one at a time . . . and thus hierarchical organizations developed.

This way of doing work is appropriate for industrial modes of production, where work is divided up, sometimes among thousands of people. Each person does the assigned work and then moves the product down or up the assembly line to the next person. The industrial mode of production, based on division of labor and central command, is still characteristic of most organizations.

In a situation where work flows from one person to another, each person becomes responsible for a particular function. Efficiencies come by better management of that flow . . . a job of the management of the organization, not the workers. This model, taken from manufacturing where division of labor is the norm, is not suited for knowledge work, where the efficiency of work increases as collaboration becomes a reality.

An integrated digital environment is based on information sharing, making what I produce available to others who need it – freely and openly.
The values implicit in an integrated digital environment enable a more productive approach and require a transformed work culture.
In such a work culture:

- Information sharing replaces information hoarding.
- Horizontal relationships become more important than vertical relationships.
- Every staff member – regardless of rank or position – knows the "health of the fleet" and the impact of his or her Work on it.
- Cooperation and collaboration are essential for success in the Knowledge Age.

Knowledge work, community of practice and integrated digital environment are concepts that help us understand the new work culture that is needed for knowledge work. We turn now to how we can bring about such a work culture.

CHAPTER 6

Communities of Practice

The term "community practice" comes for the world of learning theory. The term helps us understand the context in which knowledge work is done. It was introduced through a collaboration of a computer technologist focusing on artificial intelligence, and an anthropologist. Etienne Wenger, the intelligent tutoring expert, says that he believes that the anthropologist Jean Lave first used the term community of practice. She says, however that Wenger invented the term. In any case, Lave and Wenger best capture the meaning of the term community of practice.

Wenger, who has written most extensively on the term, describes a community of practice as follows:

> *"We all belong to communities of practice. At home, at work, at school, in our hobbies – we belong to several communities at any given time."*[49]

What interests us here is how the concept enlightens our understanding of knowledge work. Wenger says,

---

[49] Etienne Wenger, Communities of Practice. Learning, Meaning and Identity. Cambridge: Cambridge University Press, 1998, p. 6. A decade before they wrote Communities of Practice, Lave and Wagner collaborated on a brilliant little book on apprenticeships in which they articulated the essential components of the concept. Lave and Wenger, Situated Learning. Legitimate Peripheral Participation. Cambridge 1991.

> *Workers organize their lives with their immediate colleagues and customers to get their jobs done. In doing so, they develop or preserve a sense of themselves they can live with, have some fun, and fulfill their requirements and clients."[50]*

From the viewpoint of the individual worker, this is valid, but it is unwise to think that "workers organize their lives." In reality, their lives are generally organized for them. In the industrial mode of production, the organization designs down to the tiniest detail of the work life. The technical environment also "organizes" our lives. The tools we have, the machines that enable us to do our work, determine how we do that work.

An integrated digital environment opens up new opportunities and tools for workers to "organize their lives" and increase their productivity. Wenger points out that,

> *No matter what their official job description may be, they create a practice to do what needs to be done. Although workers may be contractually employed by a large institution, in day-to-day practice they work with – and in a sense, for – a much smaller set of people and communities."[51]*

What Wenger describes is a community of practice, which is a key element in which we call the work culture – the assumptions that people bring to work with them.

Knowledge work, as we have seen, is collaborative in nature. It is shared. In order to understand how knowledge is created and how knowledge is shared, we need to look at the concept of community of practice.

Communities, as we use the term, are groups of people who work for a common purpose within an organization, or across organizational boundaries. The community is an environment in which work takes place. Such communities are not restricted to a geographical area, but are connected by their common history and work goals.

In the previous chapter we saw that knowledge work is the creative process that gives us answers to questions – "Is it a good idea to . . . ?" These answers are judgments – and if we claim that they are knowledge statements, then we have what philosophers call a "justified true belief."

The work to come to our judgments and beliefs takes place within communities. These communities may be highly formal with settled and

---

50 Ibid.
51 Ibid.

> **Information is a Living Activity**
> *Information is a living activity. The information revolution is based on the fundamental fact that the value of information grows with use rather than disappears. Information, unlike other resources, is not depletable. When information is passed on to someone else, rather than being lost, depleted, or "given away, " it is shared and its uses multiply. The more it is used, manipulated, and connected to other information, the more value it takes on.*[52]

organized bodies or knowledge or they may be informal communities with little structured bodies of knowledge. Knowledge management theorists and practitioners call these communities of practice – communities united by a common work and a body of knowledge.

Knowledge arises not out of the particular activity of one person, but the collective work of the community. The conditions for collaboration are created in communities of practice. Of course, an individual is the source of knowledge, but the development of a body of knowledge and how any particular part of that body fits with the whole, takes place within a community. Knowledge is not just a piece, but part of a whole picture of reality.

We need a new language for this sort of resource – a resource that grows as it is used, both in quantity and in value. We know about depletable resources, like oil; about renewable resources, like corn. But there are other resources that appreciate over time and with use – like money well invested, a well-worn Persian carpet, energy devoted to rearing a healthy child, or like information shared within a community and with other communities. Perhaps we should call these transformable resources. The use and reuse of resources is part of the care necessary to the nurturing of a knowledge community.

Information exchange is at the heart of the work community. Information, as it grows and prospers, takes on additional meaning and life. As information is handled by one creative mind and then another within a community, new ideas are added, new insights gained, new uses derived – value is added to information in its use, reuse and exchange. Knowledge is created. And those who shared their knowledge are enriched in the process. Knowledge grows in a community.

---

[52] Ken Megill et. al. Making the information revolution. Washington, DC: Association for Information and Image Management, 1995. pp. 14–15.

The concept of community of practice is one of the keys to understanding the nature of work in the Knowledge Age. Because work takes place in groups informally bound to one another, it is through exposure to a common class of problems, common pursuit of solutions, and a store of common knowledge, that knowledge is created.

Community

Communities are our "home" – the place where we can take off our shoes and do our best work. Creativity best comes within a community . . . and as communities intersect.

The term "community" comes from sociology and anthropology. In these disciplines, a community is defined as groups of any size whose members reside in a specific locality, share a government, and have a common cultural and historical heritage. A community is united by a shared set of values (a culture, assumptions about how we live) and these values are, in most cases, developed over time in a particular geographic area.

Even though this term has a relatively short history, first being introduced by Lave and Wenger in 1992, it taps into a long tradition, especially in the scientific community where the notion of community is widely used in American pragmatism. The American philosopher, Charles Sanders Peirce, spoke eloquently and often about the community of scientific enquirers and said that truth was what, in the long run, that community will believe. This use of community, like that of Wenger and Lave, does not rely on geographical proximity, but grows out of a common history and work – they are defined by the knowledge they share.

Definition of Community

"A community can be a collection of people who share something in common . . . A collection of people who share a geographical territory and some measure of interdependency that provides the reason for living in the same space." Allan G. Johnson, Blackwell Dictionary of Sociology, 1995, pp. 48–49. Charles Winick in the Dictionary of Anthropology (Philosophical Library, 1956, p. 126) defines community as "mutually dependent families living and working together in a given area and usually in face-to-face association."

In a digital age a community is not restricted by the necessity to move information captured and stored in physical form (such as documents, letters, books, articles, etc.) from place to place. The digital age enables us to live and work in "virtual" communities that otherwise exhibit all the other characteristics of a community.

> *"Communities of Practice" is a phrase coined by researchers who studied the ways in which people naturally work and play together. In essence, communities of practice are groups of people who share similar goals and interests. In pursuit of these goals and interests, they employ common practices, work with the same tools and express themselves in a common language. Through such common activity, they come to hold similar beliefs and value systems." Community Intelligence Labs. http://www.co-i-l. com/coil/knowledge-garden/cop/definitions.shtml*

As we have said before, knowledge workers live and work in a number of communities, some more important than others – and much of their creativity comes from the intersections of the communities that come together to perform work. Different communities have different sets of values, understandings and common sense, so when they intersect, tensions often arise. Out of these tensions often comes creativity – or, when there is not an openness to other communities – strife.

We work in communities – often several at the same time. And we work with people who live, physically and professionally, in very different communities.

Biologists and chemists were once in very different fields, but great progress came in human knowledge when the field of biochemistry emerged. Mathematicians and physicists sometimes share the insights of poets and theologians as new ways of thinking about the true nature of the universe emerge. Knowledge often comes from unexpected places – and unexpected connections. If we know the answer, then we can let the machine do the work – process the data, find the correlations, make a copy, send a fax and create a microfilm copy all at the same time. Knowledge is about answer questions that we don't know how to answer – this is the process of discovering if it is a good idea to do . . . .

Indeed, creativity emerges – and grows – through the interaction and interfaces of communities in the work place.

The development of knowledge work and communities of practice gives us the possibility for a new work culture. We can begin to envision – and perhaps even understand the kind of work culture that is appropriate for knowledge work.

Ba

The Japanese led the way as they brought the notion of "ba" (community) and cooperation to the assembly line. They showed that automation is most effective when done in cooperation with the work force. The Japanese pioneered the concept and use of quality circles to focus on the customer and the product.

A next logical step is the use the concept of "Ba," as it has been used by Ikujiro Nonaka. Ba goes beyond cooperation to collaboration. "Ba" describes the environment in which work takes place. The interactions to which Nonaka refers imply collaboration. Collaboration is more than sharing. It is working together.

He emphasizes that it is very important that management work hard to make sure that the proper "Ba" is nurtured. Ba is the context that makes a safe haven for the creation of knowledge (that intangible, boundary-less, dynamic creation of the human mind in interaction with other human minds)[53].

Ba, Nonaka says, harbors meaning. Ba is a theory that the Japanese know clearly. It is a very important concept in Japanese social life. It represents both place and situation, plus context with all the relationships included. Ba is the lodging place, the shelter, which contains meaning.

Nonaka focuses on the process of knowledge creating a knowledge transfer:

"Knowledge creation and knowledge transfer" (are) "delicate processes, necessitating particular forms of support and 'care'

A Japanese View of Ba

"Your role in Japanese society changes according to "ba." If I behave without knowing in what context I am speaking or acting, I might be regarded to be: strange, rude, conceited, foolish or childish. There is frequent checking on and correction to behaving appropriate to each situation. It was often confusing as different people have different criteria for 'rightness'."[54]

---

[53] Ikujiro Nonaka and Toshihiro Nishiguchi. Knowledge Emergence: Social, Technical, and Evolutionary Dimensions of Knowledge Creation. Oxford: Oxford University Press, 200. Ibid. 18–19
[54] Personal Communication to Evie Lotze from Yositko Higuchi

from management . . . . Knowledge must be 'nurtured' rather than managed."[55]

"The Ba must be attended, nurtured. I.e. the context, the community, the safe harbor for creating knowledge work, must be attended to.

"The most important aspect of ba is 'interaction' . . . Ba is the space where such interactions take place." "Ba is a space-time Nexus or, as Heidegger put it, a locationality that simultaneously includes space and time"

"Knowledge is embedded in ba, where it is then acquired through one's own experience of reflections on the experiences of others. If knowledge is separated from ba it turns into information."[56]

An individual knowledge worker is part of multiple communities, and is therefore negotiating the norms and relationships of various "Ba". Rather than import the Japanese word, elegant though the concept is, we have incorporated its meaning into our own thinking about Communities of Practice.

Practice/Praxis

The term community, from sociology and anthropology, is one of the key terms in "community of practice." The other is that of practice/praxis that is a philosophical notion used to describe the process of applying a body of knowledge in work. It is the process of taking data and information and making it into knowledge.

Praxis/Practice is the activity of work that combines physical and intellectual labor. It is the fundamental human activity. It is what makes humans what we are. For the knowledge worker, practice/praxis is the transformation of information into knowledge . . . it is real work. It is not ruled by the machine or the state of the technology.

We speak, for example, of the "practice of medicine" or the "legal practice" – a way of doing something that emerges out of a combination of knowledge learned from a body of knowledge and "practical" experience.

---

[55] Knowledge Emergence. Social, Technical and Evolutionary Dimensions of Knowledge Creation. Edited by Ikujiro Nonaka and Toshiro Nishiguchi, Oxford 2001, p. 4
[56] ibid. p. 19

PRAXIS

In the European traditions, the term "praxis" is used. Germans use "praxis" for the "business" lawyers and doctors maintain; it compre-hends all their clients and all the work they do for their clients. Praxis includes more than the English verb to practice, it includes customs and cultural content, as well. Praxis is often translated as "practice" in English, but it comes with very different overtones. Praxis implies a combination of theory and action. The person most clearly identified with articulating the notion of praxis is Karl Marx, especially his early writings that were written in the 1840's and discovered in the 1920's. His writings on praxis and alienation infused generations of thinking about work and the nature of work.

The term practical is at the heart of American pragmatism. It has many formulations that boil down to the statement: "if you want to know what something means, then you need to know its practical effects. If there are no practical effects then it is meaningless." Since 1878, when Peirce first[57] used the maxim, pragmatism has become woven into the American world outlook.

Thinking about something and changing it in practical ways appear to be two different activities – in fact, they are an iterative process. In knowledge work, thought and activity come together to transform the world. The marriage of thought and activity helps us understand the nature of that transformation.

Being practical means that what we do makes a difference. It is closely tied to the concept of work, although that linkage was seldom made in the pragmatic tradition.

Most communities do not need to be created. They already exist or merely "come about." Communities of practice do, however, need to be identified and nurtured in order for knowledge work to be done effectively and efficiently. Identifying and making accessible the knowl-edge of a community is one of the most important activities of knowledge management.

The development of various collaborative tools makes it possible for bodies of knowledge to be made accessible in new and interesting ways. Much of the power of web technology resides in its ability to make the

---

[57] Popular Science Monthly, January 1878, (xii. 287). Peirce says that he first used the concept in the Revue philosophique VII, (Collected Papers, 5.19)

Key Attributes of a Collaborative Community of Practice
The community shares a unifying purpose. Information/Knowledge about the work, service, or the unifying purpose is openly shared.

- Major portions of the community's work can be accomplished within an integrated digital environment with participant's utilizing software applications with common functionality that share files.
- All the players/workers can access the software applications and work together on-line.
- The community's supporting systems have been integrated much like a dot.com to support the collaborative environment.
- Training is on-line and integrated into the business practices.
- Community knowledge can be collected, organized, and shared within the software applications – expert system. On-line reference libraries of applicable documents can be built and maintained.
- Members of the community can communicate using many different methods including text, chat, audio, video, shared whiteboard, on-line meetings, as well as shared or entirely different applications.
- There are self-evident benefits to the individuals within the community to cause them to use the software environment.
- Innovation is encouraged and supported.

People have work related identities in both their operational "homes" as well as within various types of work related communities. People engage in creative discussions with those from fields that intersect their own in real and virtual communities nurtured by policies that support collaboration, rewards geared to team efforts, and supported by enabling technologies and archivists who will store and keep current the information produced in knowledge work.

---

knowledge of members of a community available to others without going through an exhaustive publication process or traveling long distances for a conversation. These tools enable:

- Immediate access to the information needed to do real work.
- The automation of non-knowledge tasks – the work of the industrial mode of production is taken over by machines (and especially one kind of machine, the computer).

- Payment for production, not for time spent "at the office." Knowledge work can be done from anywhere with offices needed for face to face meetings, meetings with clients, and some sophisticated technology that is not found in homes – or on beaches.
- Management to encourage and support communities of practice, enable collaboration, support the technology necessary for workers to gain immediate access to the information they need, store and make accessible to others the knowledge they create, promote trust, risk-taking, information sharing, and working in a transparent workspace.

The drive behind knowledge management's use of the term community of practice is to increase productivity and combat the loss of the corporate memory of an organization. By automating the process of knowledge capture and retrieval, the "best practices" of an organization can be identified and replicated. The tacit knowledge of a community needs to be made explicit and organized so it can be re-used by other members of the community.

Technology Scaffold

In order for a community of practice to do its work, it requires lots and lots of tools and a "scaffold" – an integrated digital environment in which the community does its work. These tools need to be organized and be part of a business and technical architecture. The technical architecture, properly put together, gives us a road map for the wires and computers. The decisions about technical architecture are made with input from the user community.

   As we go through life . . . and our life's work . . . we enter, leave and work within various communities. Businesses and organizations develop as a part of one or more communities. They organize around specific work processes – to accomplish specific tasks. To do work.

   Communities come together and are constituted through the work done by the organizations and institutions within it . . . and by the interactions that exist among the members of the community. Communities share a body of knowledge . . . the results of their history and work. In the Knowledge Age, the primary product of work is knowledge, which is information for other knowledge workers. We can often identify work communities by the knowledge that they share.

The Baobab Tree – How One Kind of Community Shared Knowledge

Evie Lotze, Work Culture Transformation, p. 90

Traditionally the know-how (about what really gets results and which mistakes to avoid) resides mainly in people's minds. In ancient villages, the elders and early professionals like the midwife, healer, and priest passed on this knowledge through palavers under the baobab tree.

Like the elders, the Buddha sat under a tree, the Bodi tree, until he attained enlightenment. We call such an enlightened one a guru, which means one who leads from darkness into light. A guru has a clear vision and serves as a guiding light until the new reality dawns on others, as well. He went from the Bodi tree and shared what he knew to be true.

Later, in Western cultures, people met to debate and exchange the best knowledge under the trees of the village square.

Only recently have we eliminated the trees and moved indoors to town meetings that performed this same knowledge-exchange function.

In the paper-based culture, such exchanges took place at conferences, workshops, conclaves, professional consultations, and meetings – all functions that enabled individuals to share what they knew and all functions that required bringing people together in one location.

The world in which knowledge workers operate continuously changes so rapidly that waiting for the gathering of the best available knowledge at a conference, or meeting the elders under the local baobab tree is hardly practical. We need a new tree, a new way of working together that facilitates the exchange of knowledge that used to happen under the baobab tree, under the Bodi tree, around the village square, or at annual conferences.

In the Age of Knowledge, these "trees" are called communities of practice ... groups of people brought together through the work they do to capture and spread ideas and know-how in free-flowing, creative ways that foster new approaches to problems.

In the digital world, chat rooms, discussion groups, and collaborative work environments are becoming the new Baobab Tree. Emerging technologies suggest that the exchange route is the World Wide Web, the Internet. The tale of Rumpelstiltskin suggests it is communities. Growing Communities of Practice suggest that both are right.

Cultivating a Community of Practice

Communities live and exist with other communities in networks. They are "organic" in nature and can grow, develop, get sick, flourish, die and be reborn.

Communities are networks, so it is not surprising that the language of community re-emerges with new technologies that enables us to live and communicate with multiple communities.

The identification, development and nurturing of communities of practice becomes an essential task for society to appropriately and productively work in the Knowledge Age. The linking of the notions of community and practice in every-day-life is beginning and will have profound impacts in the development of our political and social culture. Understanding the nature of communities of practice begins to give us a

---

Nurturing Communities of Practice

Like gardens, they (communities of practice) respond to attention that respects their nature . . . till the soil, pull out weeds, add water during dry spells, and ensure that your plants have the proper nutrients. And while you may welcome the wildflowers that bloom without any cultivation, you may get even more satisfaction from those vegetables and flowers you started from seed. The same is true for companies that grow communities of practice from seed. To get communities going – and to sustain them over time – managers should:

Identify potential communities of practice that will enhance the company's strategic capabilities;

Provide the infrastructure that will support such communities and enable them to apply their expertise effectively;

Use nontraditional methods to assess the value of the company's communities of practice.

– Wenger and Snyder in Harvard Business Review (Jan.–Feb. 2000)

way to get our minds around work and how it is transforming.

The recognition, nurturing and development of communities of practice is an important part of work transformation. The introduction of new tools may enable dramatic changes in the way work is done, but unless the issue of work culture transformation and community nurturing is addressed directly, little change in the way work is done may occur. The path to dramatic productivity and performance improvements lies with transforming the work culture from an information-hoarding culture to a knowledge-sharing culture. The transformed work culture focuses energy on the real work of the organization versus the activities that so often consume our time. Creating an environment that integrates tools, people and productive work attitudes can bring about this transformation.

Such an environment is an integrated digital environment and we turn now to look at it more closely. But most often, the emphasis by those who use the term is on wires and computers – the digital part. The emphasis in a transformed work culture is on the environmental part first, people second and enabling tools, the digital part, third. The environment in which digital work takes place are communities of practice.

SECTION III

The Work of Changing

In which we consider the work of those who want to create a new culture of work for the Knowledge Age.

We shall return to our friend Tom Sawyer, who understands that the best work is playful.

We have shown that all work is becoming knowledge work as professionals become workers and manual workers become professionals. We have seen how collaboration is one of the major characteristics of knowledge work.

Then we explored the concepts of knowledge work, communities of practice, and integrated digital environment.

We are now able to sketch out the new work culture that is developing

Developing the new work culture requires a new theory – a way to think about things – and new practice – experiments, trials, new institutions in real life.

It also requires a methodology of transformation.

And, finally, we note that work culture transformation takes place one person at a time and point to a companion book to understand that process.

Key Terms . *(See Glossary for more)*

Abduction – A form of logic to describe the process of creating knowledge.

Faceting – A way of describing information that focuses on uses and potential uses and the context information will be used, rather than the content of an information container, such as a book or article.

Hermeneutics (Theory of Understanding) – The methodology to interpret texts, particularly sacred texts.

Spiral Development – A methodology that accepts the fact that we cannot plan and lay out exactly where we are going and need to work in spirals.

CHAPTER 7

Work Becomes Play

"Tom said to himself that it was not such a hollow world after all . . . . If he had been a great and wise philosopher, like the writer of this book, he would now have comprehended that Work consists of whatever a body is obliged to do and that Play consists of whatever a body is not obliged to do."

Mark Twain. The Adventures of Tom Sawyer. Chapter II: "The Glorious Whitewasher."[58]

"But how is it that some people enjoy spending a great deal of time in my company . . . It is because they enjoy hearing me examine those who think that they are wise when they are not – an experience which has its amusing side."

Socrates, Apology (19c)

---

[58] For those who have forgotten (or never read) Tom Sawyer, let's set the stage for this quote. Aunt Polly, Tom's keeper and guide in life, put Tom to work on a beautiful Saturday morning. "At this dark and hopeless moment an inspiration burst upon him! Nothing less than a great, magnificent inspiration." He decided to turn work into play. When one of his colleagues came by, he allowed him to paint, after some persuasion because "Does a boy get a chance to whitewash a fence every day?" Tom had his call to adventure. By the end of the day the fence is whitewashed and Tom has walked away with many valuable objects as the various boys came by and paid him for the privilege to paint the fence. When asked, "Why, ain't that work?" he says, "Well, maybe it is, and maybe it ain't. All I know is, it suits Tom Sawyer." One moral of the story is that our attitude (work culture) shapes whether a task is work or play.

At the front of this book, we put the above quotations from Mark Twain, speaking through Tom Sawyer, and Plato, speaking through Socrates.

These two observers of human life captured the essence of work and knowledge. For both of them, the kind of work we call knowledge work is fun – something we are not obliged to do.

As we turn our attention to how we create this new environment, assuming that is what we want to do, we need to keep the thoughts of Mark Twain and Plato in mind.

Tom (who spoke for Mark Twain) did not use the proper definition of work=force x distance. But then Tom skipped a lot of school and learned life rather than physics.

Tom understood that all labor is forced labor in the world in which he was growing up. The industrial revolution was getting off to a rip-roaring start along the Mississippi River where he learned life. Work, if it was work, was forced. School was a preparation for the work world. Tom Sawyer's rebellion against that world captured the essence of humanity – what really counts is how much I get to play.

The outlines are emerging of what that life might be like when we accept and promote knowledge work. Decisions need to be made by many people, both leaders and followers, to promote an environment appropriate for knowledge work. These decisions are the essence of what makes up the work culture . . . the rules that govern the communities in which we work.

The drive to a new culture comes from new tools we use to do our work – tools that enable us to manage, transmit and share information. It enables us to free our work from a particular space and (often) a particular time.

Playing is at the heart of knowledge work. Creativity and play often merge – and the emergence of knowledge work means that we are faced with a nice new problem – how do we free people to play – to take risks, to create new toys, to put together things in unique new ways, to make up rules as they go along, to be inventive??

So we come back to Socrates – the Hemlock Drinker. Knowledge workers need to adopt the attitude of questioning that he displayed in both his theory and practice. He described himself as a stinging fly:[59]

---

[59] For those who have forgotten (or never read) Plato, let's set the stage for this quote. Socrates is speaking to his fellow citizens in Athens. He is on trial for his life, accused of corrupting the youth. The report of his trial, called the Apology, was written by Plato. Socrates, himself, was a great teacher and thinker, but never wrote. He left that to his student, Plato. In the end, Socrates was convicted and sentenced to drink the poison, hemlock, which he did – his students at his side.

"It is literally true, even if it sounds rather comical, that God has specially appointed me to this city, as though it were a large thoroughbred horse which because of its great size is inclined to be lazy and needs the stimulation of some stinging fly. It seems to me that God has attached me to this city to perform the office of such a fly, and all day long never cease to settle here, there, and everywhere, rousing, persuading, reproving every one of you." (Apology, 30(e))

It was Socrates who first asked, and answered, the question – what is knowledge? It is justified true belief, what we know works, what makes sense. The information created by others and ourselves that we bring to bear on our lives and our work.

Knowledgeable people like to be around those who make knowledge. It is their fun, their amusement. As Socrates explained to his accusers: "But how is it that some people enjoy spending a great deal of time in my company? You have heard the reason, gentlemen; I told you quite frankly. It is because they enjoy hearing me examine those who think that they are wise when they are not – an experience which has its amusing side." (Apology 33(c))

Human beings as works in process are animated by dreams of a better life, and by utopian longings for fulfillment.[60] Is it any wonder that in a culture in which people spend 40–60 hours of a week trying to figure out how to make work less onerous and working many of the dreams for a better life revolve around ways to get out of work and, sometimes, to transform that work? Much of our hope for a better life includes the hope that our work can be filled with meaning and reward. That it can be "elevated work," work that makes a difference, work that at the end passes the "so what?" test. Work that lets us answer with pride the "What will you do with your one un-replaceable life time?" question. Thinking for a living seems to be a desirable goal for many as it holds the possibility of replacing a life of drudgery with one of creativity.

When we bring our full one-pointed focus onto our work, make meditation of it, we re-enter the child-like state of play. When we bring our creativity and the power of our imagination to bear on a work problem, we again enter the childhood realm of play.

Play is the way children prepare to enter the adult world. It is the serious work of childhood. Children try on roles, they learn the rules of games

---

[60] Ernst Bloch's, (German philosopher) The Principle of Hope, provides an exhaustive examination of the ways that daydreams, fairy tales and myths, popular culture, literature, theater, and all forms of art, political and social utopias, philosophy, and religion contain "emancipatory moments" that project visions of a better life.

that help them to gain mastery, they practice skills, and they invent worlds and enter them whole-heartedly. They know with the openness of a childhood mind that they are not the "ones who know," not yet. They are still open. Their cup is not so full it can hold no more. As we enter a new Age of Knowledge, what better quality could we hope to bring to it?

For in the end – and at the beginning – life is about Work – and work is about play.

Tom Sawyer got it right.

CHAPTER 8

The Nature of Knowledge Work: Thinking Spirally

So – how do we think playfully and playfully think? How do we actually do this new kind of work? How do we get our mind around how we can carry out our lives in meaningful ways as industrial modes of production are replaced by a transformed work culture? What are the methodologies that we can use as we do our knowledge work? How do we think about our new way to do work?

Many thinkers have struggled to define this new way to approach work. One of the most interesting ways to look at work is to focus on its spiral nature. We could – and no doubt will – use other language and other ways to describe the new work culture we are in the process of building. But thinking about spiral development gives us one way to get a new kind of common sense.

The new work culture brings with it a new sense of time and space which is very different that the one where many of us learned the meaning of work. The work that goes into the making of knowledge is inherently creative – it involves the creation of something new – qualitatively new within systems and context. One way of understanding how this work is done is spiral development, the methodology most widely used within the software development community.

The work culture of the knowledge age requires a very different view of the world. We need a theory that expresses how we do knowledge work.

Part of this new theory involves "systems thinking" – looking at the world and work in terms of systems, with feedback and understanding within a context. This way of thinking underpins the introduction of computer technologies into the work place. The work of software development is, perhaps, one of the best examples of knowledge work, for it is how the computer is instructed to act and do its tasks.

Spiral production – that appropriate to knowledge work – is done in digital "space" and "time." Spiral development is collaborative in nature and requires a high level of interaction among the members of a community. Like other collaborative work, where appropriate technology is used, it does not necessarily require spatial and temporal contiguity.

Software Development[61]

When computers were first invented and software programs were written, the software developers adopted the ways of work appropriate for the industrial mode of production. Their way of work was taken from project management that assumes that either the developers or the people for whom the product/tool is being developed know what is needed and how the needs can be met.

Once the user's needs are identified by a needs analysis, the requirements to meet those needs are codified. A schedule is then laid out to develop software that met those requirements. The schedule often covers many years with many stages. The software developer "manages" the project through its various stages, with one stage being completed before moving onto the next. Work tasks are broken into pieces, divided up among workers and coordinated and organized by management. The development of software is put on an assembly line.

Prior to the development of the spiral methodology software development proceeded like a waterfall – from stage to stage. And, like a waterfall, once you start going over it, changes in direction or speed are nearly impossible – changes in direction or speed are dictated by the waterfall, not controlled by the one falling. The spiral methodology is an attempt to avoid getting caught in an irreversible stream of events.

A recurring problem with many technology implementation projects is

---

[61] The author is indebted to Noel Dickover and Charlie Montague, two practitioners involved in software development. The description here is simple-minded and shaped to the theme of work culture transformation, but captures, I hope, the essence of what they taught me.

the continually changing requirements over the course of the project. As the implementation progresses, a number of factors are generally referred to as the "requirements creep":

The initial set of requirements that drove the implementation was not clear – or they changed. The understanding of the problem evolves – either because we understand more as we go along or our world changes. As our understanding evolves, the requirements are modified

The technologists and developers often become isolated from actual users, and end up with different priorities than the users. A more conceptually effective way of developing software is now the norm – it is called spiral development. A spiral replaces the traditional assembly line method.

We cannot plan and lay out exactly where we are going. We may think we can, but we need to be prepared for changes. As soon as we get to one stage, new technologies provide new challenges and new possibilities for the succeeding stages.

The primary impetus for spiral development, like most ways to think differently about work, is driven by very practical considerations. It is simply impossible, given the pace of technological development, to plan and know how a complex project will develop because the very act of creativity makes a new world. In other words, the requirements for the "end state" – the finished system – cannot be completely described, no matter how we try. It is impossible to know the exact requirements because they often change over time. Technology advances create new opportunities that drive development and a change within one part of a system impacts the entire system.

Failures

The world of information technology is littered with failed systems.

There are many reasons why most information technology projects fail. Organizations sometimes attempt to meet an environment where change is endemic by continually shifting and redesigning the organizational lines of communication. Failures, it is said, are a result of "poor communications" so communication paths are reconfigured. The continual changing of organizational structures leads to a jaded work environment that is reactive rather than proactive. Reorganizations take the place of transformation.

Instead of accepting the reality of a change in the work place, hope is often placed in technology to solve the problems encountered in the work place. Political decisions truncate or deflect attempts to transform the work place. Decisions and actions in organizations have a shorter and shorter life span. Short-term decisions, if they don't take place in a structure that supports flexibility, lead to long-term problems, instability, and ineffective and inefficient work.

Often the responsibility for failure is laid on either the user or the developer, but not on the lack of collaboration between the developer and the customer. The attitude often is "How do we get better users?" or "why can't we get a developer who can listen and understand?" rather than on "Why aren't we building products that meets the real needs?"

Blaming the customer and the work culture is often the last (and sometimes desperate) attempt by information technology folks to explain why the expected benefits do not flow from their technologies. Changing a work culture is often about changing expectations that people bring to their work, as much as building more and better information systems.

In environments that are rapidly changing, structured organizations have problems adapting to changes in communications, supplier operations, required skill sets, customer expectations, and technology options.

These failures are a result of the inability or unwillingness to confront the necessity of change in the work culture . . . to look at new ways of doing work. The industrial model of work fails in the knowledge age because it cannot achieve what it sets out to do. It cannot finish what it starts. The project changes before it reaches the original finish line. The true needs of the user, which may be different from what they want or say they want, cannot be known prior to the beginning the creative process. Focusing on "use cases" – how the software will actually be used helps get a handle on the work that needs to be done. Use cases become the requirements – they are called "use stories."

The nature of creative/knowledge work is that the outcome cannot be predicted in advance because creative work transforms the situation and creates a new reality.

We Don't Know the End

The spiral development way of thinking starts with the proposition that we do not know where the project will end . . . no matter how hard we work to define all of the variables and take all of the "wrinkles" out of the process.

No longer can software developers tell people how to do their business. The successful software developer must meet the business needs of an organization that are necessarily specialized and in flux.

Software is not developed from scratch. Previously, many organizations controlled the requirements, and could build exactly what they thought they wanted. Now, however, instead of building products and software from scratch, people integrate components. The world is more complex, and the options for creating software are more diversified. The real driving force in software development is the needs of the customer – the use of the product determines its development. To be done effectively and efficiently, the customer's needs must be taken into consideration throughout the software development process.

The spiral methodology moves problems and risks to the beginning of the development process. The focus is on answering what is not known first, not what is known, which enables change to be built into the process from the beginning. When we start this work we have an idea where we are going, but the picture may change as we go forward. Spiral development accommodates change.

The customer needs to "play" with the products as they are created – to see how they fit into the work and how work processes can be transformed to take full advantage of the technology as it develops. This interchange between the customer and the developers proceeds in a spiral like fashion. Most problems are complex enough that they are rarely understood in one setting through one perspective, let alone from all of the appropriate perspectives.

Instead of exerting energy on refining requirements and building something to meet it, extensive effort is now spent on researching what is available to meet "generalized" needs of a community. The software developer, who is one kind of knowledge worker, works collaboratively with the software user in order to invent new knowledge.

Agility

Some of the proponents of the new way to develop software call this way of doing work agile. Agile proponents advocate that development occur in smaller, tight spirals. The overall development process of analyze, design, develop, implement and support repeats in smaller development efforts. Instead of developing final requirements, the agile proponents develop to only what they know and understand. Development spirals are built on top of previous ones. Over time, a quasi-final product emerges which supports user needs. Development is an on-going process, agile enough to evolve with the changing nature of the work.

Some agile technologies advocate the use of two programmers working in unison to develop a single set of code. This collaborative approach,

> "Extreme Programming is a discipline of software development with values of simplicity, feedback and courage. We focus on the roels of customer, manager, and programmer and accord key rights and responsibilities to those in those roles." One textbook describing the spiral process is Royce, Walker. Software Project Management, A Unified Framework. Reading Mass: Addison-Wesley. 1998.

first advocated by Extreme Programming, integrates the requirements and coding process together as a single work task. Two software programmers work together in unison – one doing the coding and the other ensuring that the coding matches the previously developed requirements and test plan. While sitting side by side, one programmer is always focused on the user requirements, while the other is doing the actual coding. Test plans are written jointly prior to coding. This is far different from the traditional model, in which requirements are handed to an individual programmer, who, working individually only comes back when that piece is complete. The work is done together, even though each person may be focusing on a particular part of the work process. In order for this way of work to function, it is necessary for everyone to have an understanding of the entire process and how the various pieces fit together.

To effectively engage in the agile process, great care is spent attempting to build flexibility into the coding process. We start with a goal in mind, but we start with an understanding that the software will change. Instead of optimizing the software for today, the goal is to allow the software to grow into tomorrow's requirements. This requires what is called a "flexible architecture."

This approach to software development meets the needs of today's work culture. Using the approach, software is adaptive instead of adapted. The user's (customer's) needs drive development. A work culture based on open communication, trust, and collective responsibility can work towards recognizing and making the changes necessary to survive over longer time frames.

Designing for Flexibility

The "current reality" is short-term. The world will continue to change – technology will continue to evolve, customers will continue to have changing expectations, theories on management will continue to be refined, etc.

To adapt quickly to change, the organization must know what it is offering, how it is currently conducting business, and how this impacts the larger environment. There must be an on-going analysis on the part of the organization, through its communities of practice, to determine how well it currently matches the larger environment's need.

Creating structures that survive and flourish over an extended duration, organizations should begin to understand the parts of their organization that are relatively stable and the parts which are more transient in nature. The parts that are relatively stable should be structured loosely to allow maximum collaboration and interaction among the affected stakeholders. The parts of the organization that are relatively transient in nature should be segregated in such a way that they are easy to replace. In software development terms, we would call this a "component."

Components in software are cordoned off into their own code, and have strictly controlled communications with the rest of the application. If a component (a discussion tool, for instance) needs to be changed or upgraded, it can be replaced without affecting the rest of the application. The interface . . . the communication among the elements . . . is what is preserved. Components are stable, but the "insides" of components can change and the components can be a useful part of a system.

Three Philosophical Theories for Knowledge Work

This same principle – focusing on interfaces and communication with work being done within and by communities in a way that it can be changed to meet the needs of the users of knowledge – is essential for effective knowledge work.

In organizational terms, this means smaller, integrated units versus large scale, end-to-end processes. Smaller, integrated components, while not always be as profitable or high performing in the short run are far easier to change or replace. Over time, a significant savings or performance improvement can be realized.

Philosophers often foresee the development of new ways of thinking long before they enter into our common sense. Some of the philosophical concepts that help us understand the nature of knowledge work include:

* The process of hermeneutics, now a major force in philosophy throughout the Western world, and
* The theory of abduction developed by the American philosopher C.S. Peirce, as well as

• The theory of faceting, one of the significant contributions in the field of library science.

These are three different ways to view and articulate the rising new work culture.

These theories each present ways to understand reality that are at odds with what was once our common sense – the culture that underlay and infused our work in the industrial era. They can help us get our minds around our new work culture.

Back to Understanding (Hermeneutics)

Hermeneutics is the art and science of understanding.[62] It is perhaps most clearly explained in the works of Hans Georg Gadamer who developed some of the insights of the phenomenologist[63] who dominated continental philosophy in the middle and end of the twentieth century. It is perhaps best known from theology, where hermeneutics is the art/science of understanding and interpreting scripture. The methodology, however, has a much broader application.

Understanding is a fundamentally different process than explanation. Understanding takes place in a context . . . in a community. Other philosophers, such as Wittgenstein, Husserl, and Whitehead, share this insight.

For our discussion, the concept of "knowledge" as we use it is closely related to "understanding" – a process that has a different character than

---

[62] The author is indebted to Karl-Otto Apel, with whom he studied in 1961–62 when Professor Apel, then a Privat Dozent, presented a seminar on Gadamer (as well as one on Peirce). Apel understands the fundamental unity underlying the pragmatic and hermeneutical traditions. His student (and dear friend of the author) Gerd Wartenberg translated Peirce into German and developed many of the concepts in this book many years ago in the realm of social work and educational theory prior to his untimely death.

[63] The phenomenologists were a philosophical school that matured and had great influence in the middle of the twentieth century – particularly in the non-English speaking parts of Europe. Phenomenology is described as: "Description of experience. Hence, a philosophical method restricted to careful analysis of the intellectual processes of which we are introspectively aware, without making any assumptions about their supposed causal connections to existent external objects. Philosophers who have made extensive use of diverse phenomenological methods include Brentano, Husserl, Hartmann, Heidegger, and Merleau-Ponty." A Dictionary of Philosophical Terms and Names. http://www.philosophypages.com/dy/index.htm This is the same tradition that Wenger uses for his concept of community of practice and Nonake refers to in his discussion of "Ba".

merely explaining something. Knowledge requires coming to terms with and getting "inside" the object of knowledge.

Hermeneutics focuses on understanding texts, rather than explaining them. The process of understanding requires us to recognize that we all have pre-judgments (or prejudices) that come out of our previous understanding and the communities in which we live.

Understanding is always from a point of view and can never be "objective" in the sense of looking at a set of circumstances without judgments that are already formed.

Making knowledge is, at root, a process of understanding what is going on. It requires determining that one's beliefs are justified by experience and evidence. The process of understanding – making knowledge – is inherently social. Understanding grows out of the historical and cultural situation in which work is done in communities.

Making knowledge – doing knowledge work – involves bringing information together, synthesizing it, criticizing it and coming to a new and deeper understanding.

Understanding is a qualitative activity – with understanding that "deepens" and is "better" than what one knew before.

Making knowledge is a matter of understanding what is going on and making the case so others can come to an understanding.

Abduction

A nineteenth century American philosopher, Charles Sanders Peirce, gives us a concept, abduction, which can help us understand the nature of knowledge work. Peirce was grounded in scientific work and logic. Logic describes how thinking is done. Most of us are familiar with the concepts of induction and deduction, which we use regularly in the process of thinking. Peirce introduces a third term, abduction, that is more appropriate for knowledge creation.

Peirce is best known for articulating and describing pragmatism – the quintessential American philosophy. He later called his philosophy pragmaticism to distinguish it from the popularized version of his views. He spent much of his time probing the nature of logic – how we think. He pondered about how we can deduct particulars from a general truth (deduction) and general statements from particulars (induction) – and noticed that these two forms of logic are not sufficient to describe how we think.

Deduction is the favorite form of logic for those who want certainty. Deductive reasoning relies on the assumed truth of previous conclusions and deduces other conclusions because of premises. Deduction enables us to get a particular truth from other, general, truths.

A typical example of deductive reasoning is:

All men are mortal.
Harry is a man.
Therefore, Harry is mortal.

The conclusion follows with certainty from the first two statements.

Induction, on the other hand, does not bring us certainty. The conclusion of inductive reasoning gives us probability, for it relies on particular instances that may be counter indicated later.

An example of inductive reasoning is:

Harry Smith is bald.
Harry James is bald.
Harry Easter is bald.
Harry Pape is bald.
Harry Brown is bald.
Therefore, all Harry's are bald.

The conclusion comes from a number of instances and, depending on the quality and scope of the observations, can often approach certainty. In fact, if these are all of the Harry's in the world, then we could conclude that all of them are bald, based on our observation. Of course, it takes just one Harry with hair to make the conclusion no longer valid.

Induction enables us to create new "truths" but these truths suffer from a significant flaw – they do not bring certainty to our conclusions – and we know that knowledge requires certainty, a least enough certainty so we can act.

Deduction is richer in one sense for it brings certainty. Induction is richer in another way. It enables us to acquire "new" knowledge through observation and generalization and achieve "enough" certainty to act.

Inductive reasoning relies on probability – and some of Peirce's most impressive work is in the exploration of probability and how we can get enough certainty to act.

Both induction and deduction are used regularly as we do knowledge work. But Peirce perceived that induction and deduction are not enough to understand how we make knowledge. They both work fine, within defined systems, but scientific discoveries (and we would say all creative work, such as knowledge work) involve another very different process – one he calls abduction.

Abduction is a process not unlike that used by the software developers to do programming – what they call spiral development.

This process is the same as that used by those using spiral development for software development. The forming of hypotheses and refining these as the development process goes on brings us to new, and often unexpected, conclusions.

Abductive reasoning enables us to achieve relative certainty and is the essence of what we have come to know as the "scientific method." (We observe, hypothesize, test, conclude and start the process all over again.) Others have called it "dialectical" reasoning.

Let us take an example from the industrial world. Henry Ford observed the process of building an automobile. He saw that there was lot of duplication of effort. He develop an hypothesis that work would go faster and the product would be better if he could simplify the tasks and have one person do only one task, again and again. He then tested his hypothesis and thus invented a new way to organize work. But he did not do it alone. He brought with him a whole culture and understanding of how work is done, observed a process and through practice developed the assembly line. A new way of work – a transformed process was invented out of, and beyond, the old.

The Community of Scientific Inquirers

Peirce recognizes – and emphasizes that the knowledge of sciences grows out of – and within – communities.

Understanding of new truths always takes place in a context. That context consists of the knowledge that others have discovered and codified in the past. Every knowledge worker stands on the shoulders of those who have gone before – even when something new may be articulated that contradicts what others have thought was true before.

Peirce says that truth is the result of the work of the community of scientific inquirers. Abduction begins with assumptions (as does deduction), but not just any assumption, but the beliefs and understandings that we "take for granted." In other places, he calls this method "critical commonsensism" – an approach that takes "common sense" and applies critical thinking to it. What we take for granted is the result of our work and serves as the backing and evidence which we have for our beliefs.

Abduction is not just about what we already know – what "everybody" in the community accepts as the truth. Neither is it a process of generalizing from a set of specific instances. Abduction is the process of reasoning and work that puts assumptions and presumptions to the test by looking at empirical reality with one eye toward finding a new truth and, in the process, supplanting the "old" truth.

Abduction is the logic of creativity, not just doing what we do now more efficiently or effectively. When one uses abductive reasoning, the starting point is sometimes called a hypothesis . . . or an idea . . . or a hunch . . . or an understanding of some kind or another. This understanding may be more or less well formulated or may simply be a set of presumptions that the worker brings to the work. Some of these assumptions/understandings are what we call culture. Other assumptions may be the results of knowledge work done by other thinkers – the information contained in a knowledge/information domain. This gives us evidence, or warrants, for our work.

Abduction is another way to describe the process of synthesis that lies at the heart of system's thinking – synthesis is more than simply collection fact and generalizing. It is more than taking a generalization and drawing conclusions. It is the process of understanding within a whole – a kind of logic that creates new judgments and products.

This process describes what we call knowledge work. Knowledge work is done out of a set of concepts and presumptions held by a community and, by applying the results of observations, gathering new information and challenging "old" knowledge. The community comes to a new understanding of the truth.

Peirce understood that abduction is a form of reasoning – a powerful way to make knowledge. Although induction and deduction are used in the course of doing knowledge work, abductive reasoning brings new knowledge. It is a way to describe spiral thinking. It is also a way to describe the process of understanding.

Faceting

More than half a century ago, in the world of library science, Ranganathan, the brilliant Indian theoretician and practitioner, recognized the impossibility of effectively laying out hierarchical structures to manage information.

Ranganathan, working from the Hindu tradition, saw that information must be "organized" and described by "facets" rather than hierarchical systems. His theory provides a way for us to understand how information in the knowledge age can be organized and accessed by and through communities, each of which sees the same information from a different perspective.

Making information accessible requires identifying not just how the creator of information uses it ... but also how the user of information will use it. As Ranganathan defined what he called the five "Laws of Library Science":[64]

- Books are for Use
- Every Reader his Book
- Every Book its reader
- Save the Time of the Reader
- Library is a Growing Organism

Information must be seen and organized from and through communities of users ... and communities of producers of knowledge and information. There is no one single way that information or knowledge can best be organized. We cannot even predict, with certainty, the value of information at the time it is created ... for that will be determined by the users. The meaning of information comes from the users, not from the creator. A creator may think of possible uses for information, but many of the most important discoveries come from using information in the most unexpected ways.

As use of information changes, the meaning of the information changes as well. The body of knowledge grows and develops and cannot be classified once and for all. This is the same process that we see in spiral development – the outcome is not known and, indeed, the outcome may change as a result of the work done in the spiral process. Meaning grows out of context ... and the classification of information in knowledge stores must reflect these changes. Ranganathan envisioned a way in which we can dynamically "organize" knowledge stores.

Ranganathan understands information in an historical and social context. He, to use a word from another tradition, "thinks historically" – or we might say he "thinks socially" about information and its uses.

It turns out that the way Ranganathan understands how to organize and make information accessible is particularly valuable when it comes to understanding how to make digital information accessible to those who need it to do their work.[65]

---

[64] Ranganathan, S. The Five Laws of Library Science. Second Edition reprinted 1988. Bangalore: Sarada Ranganathan Endowment for Library Science.

[65] The renewed interest in the application of Ranganathan's theories can be found in a Liistserv: http://groups.yahoo.com/group/facetedclassification

Previous methods of organizing information were developed in nineteenth century schema best embodied in the Dewey Decimal system and its derivative, the Library of Congress Subject Headings. These systems fail on many accounts, primarily because they do not account for the richness of user needs. These methods are based on a librarian's decision describing what a book or article is "about" and then storing the book physically next to works that are "about" the "same thing." These methods were devised to make more efficient displaying of information. The goal of "organizing" digital information for retrieval systems is to enable us to find surprising information.

Everyone who has ever browsed a library shelf knows that this schema of organization can be very powerful. As we browse a library shelf (either literally or through an "on line" catalog), we discover new and unknown sources of information. But we know that our ability to find unexpected useful information depends on the ability of the catalogers to anticipate our needs.

The arrival of web-based work enables us to do the "linking" of one object with another much more efficiently and quickly. A web[66], as opposed to a hierarchical form of organization, allows multiple accesses to the same information and does not require the creation, implementation and management of a pre-conceived set of hierarchies that are imposed on the material.

Indexing by key words is now enhanced by the ability to search the full text of documents and collections. The best retrieval systems combine the best features of indexing with full text searching, for often what a document or item is "about" is not contained in the text of the document.

The hierarchical systems of organizing information require that each object be about one thing – because, at least in the paper world, an object can only be stored in one place. It also assumes that there is a single classification that can handle all human knowledge.

Ranganathan understood that what a book or article is about depends, not just on what the book or article says, but how it is used. The meaning/purpose/content of the book or article is a result of the interrelationship of a reader and a book. Every book has its reader and every reader its book.

---

[66] Woe unto the poor spider forced to catch his food in a trap woven hierarchically, point 1 to point 2 to point 3. A web, on the other hand, is quite efficient for keeping spiders fat and happy.

Ranganathan's method of describing and organizing information called faceting. The practical implications of the theory are mostly of interest to those who are responsible for organizing large bodies of knowledge and large collections and make them accessible to readers. His extensive body of works shows how to lay out non-hierarchical information systems. Faceting focuses on the use of a book (its reader) to determine its meaning. A book (or article or any other body of knowledge) will, therefore mean very different things to very different people. Determining what something is "about" is a complex activity rooted in the use of information that grows out of communities and may be used by very different communities.

Ranganathan's work is best known to information scientists who focus on the use of his faceting theory to describe a book or object. This is an important, but only a part of his work. What he calls the laws of library science, taken together, provide us with a way to understand how we can manage knowledge:

- Books are for Use. Organizing knowledge around use, rather than the content of the knowledge, shifts the entire focus for capturing, storing and retrieving knowledge. The customer-centered focus is essential for knowledge work. Knowledge is about how it is used. Its meaning comes from use.
- Every Reader his Book. This principle replaces one that was once held by many librarians and information managers – "Books are for Preservation." Knowledge is linked to the reader, the user, not the object containing the knowledge. Meeting the needs (which sometimes coincides with what someone wants) focuses knowledge development on the needs of a community.
- Every Book its Reader. This principle replaces one held by many that "Books are for the Chosen Few. Knowledge without readers is meaningless. Knowledge serves a purpose – to answer questions that grow out of the work done within communities.
- Save the Time of the Reader. The customer of information is king. Everything in the organization must be done to meet the needs not the needs of those who work there. Ranganathan's book is a manual full of specific suggestions to improve library services. A similar approach is instructive to any organization.
- Library is a Growing Organism. The knowledge store is organic. It grows, ages and dies. It requires nurturing and use. Knowledge grows with use. Information access is the key to knowledge work. Without access and use, the store withers away.

Information is rooted in communities – not in the information itself. That means, for example, that different communities will use information in very different ways – there is no one, single meaning that enables us to categorize our information and knowledge.

Ranganathan's theories and understanding are rooted deeply in the Hindu culture and in his desire to build and create a literate and knowledgeable India. He was not only a theoretician, but also a political leader dedicated to creating a modern society out of the ruins of the British colonial empire. He points the way for us to "organize" information for use and orients us properly for knowledge work.

A colleague, on reading this description asked how a Hindu library would be organized. Are there shelves to browse? Where are the books kept? Ranganathan's books give a great deal of guidance on these questions and introduced many practices that are now common in libraries that are open to readers. The answer to the reader's question is, I think, that it depends on the temple one is in – the perception and needs of the users of the books determine their arrangement. And this arrangement may be very different for different communities. In the digital world, where we are freed from books and shelves, "arrangement" is no longer a physical task, but an activity that enables us to identify different facets that may be of interest to different communities.

Toward a New Theory

Thinking spirally is adapting a set of organizing principles to act in a work world in which the future is not set, but is created in the process of doing work. It takes as a given that things will change and sees the process of change.

This way of thinking is at the heart of systems theory, but it is also found in many other disciplines. Even though Ranganathan, Peirce, and Gadamer come from totally different disciplines, cultures, and traditions and they did not know each other's works, they have insights that help us understand the nature of knowledge work. Even though they don't use the term, they all "think spirally" – not serially. They see knowledge in context – developed out of, through and by communities. They see making knowledge to be a creative act of thinkers in a community. They help us understand the nature of knowledge – how it is created and how it can be accessed and made available. We take what they have created and apply it in an integrated digital environment.

Thinking spirally, rather than serially, is key to the new culture of work. It is a way of thinking that enables us to do our work move effectively.

The concepts of work, knowledge, and communities of practice grow directly out of these very disparate traditions. The concepts in this book are, we believe, extensions of the ways of thinking of the thinkers who have come before us.

If what we say is true (and is therefore knowledge), knowledge can come out of very different traditions and be understood in very different ways. It is in the exchange of information and knowledge that our understanding (and knowledge) of the world we live in grows.

CHAPTER 9

The Practice of Transformation:
A Three Step Plan

Transformation needs to focus on information accessibility. Making information accessible is, in fact, the key to work culture transformation.

People do know how to transform organizations. The new work culture
can, if desired, be furthered. In order for an organization to consciously
change . . . and not just be driven by forces and technologies out of their
control, they need leadership and an organizational will to transform its
work culture.

If that desire is there, then there are methodologies that can be
followed to bring about culture change. Out of the Air Force project to
create an integrated digital environment, we developed a "methodology"
to create an information-sharing environment:[67]

• Step I: Identify the Work and the Workflow.
• Step II: Identify knowledge/information produced doing the work and
  make it accessible to those who need it to do their work.
• Step III: Identify information used (or needed) to do the work and make
  it immediately accessible to you and your colleagues.

This "methodology" is in quotes, because the specifics are not as important as the fact that it is a guide to how a work culture, in a specific
setting, can be transformed.

---

[67] See the appendix for a discussion of this project.

Changing a work culture is a practical, and not just a theoretical activity. And, like all practical activity, it requires work to implement. It requires meeting the needs of a particular situation. How change comes about depends on a particular situation and its needs.

No matter how hard we try, there is no "model" for transformation, no road map, which can be developed in one work situation and be transported, part and parcel, to another. We can learn from others, but that learning merely helps us better understand our situation. The knowledge of others can be information for us – but we must make our knowledge for ourselves (and then share it with others).

The transformation of the work place is closely linked to technologies. Technology is not the transformation, but it enables the transformation.

Leadership from Above: Change from Below

There are times and places where the leadership of an organization seeks to embrace the transformation of the culture of work. In order to bring about this transformation leadership from above is required, but change itself comes from "below" – from those who do the work.

Change management is a set of theories and practices that organizations use to bring about change. Management and business practitioners rely, almost exclusively, on the presence of a dynamic leader, called in to rescue a failed company. The new manager, so the theory goes, brings a new vision and energy to the organization and a new level of accountability. This view ahs been convincingly challenged by the empirical work done by Jim Collins. He, and his tem of researchers, set out to determine what distinguishes "good" companies from "great ones – measured primarily by their stock value over a long period of time.

One of the "surprising results" of his empirical investigation is that the leader of a great organization combines "a paradoxical blend of personal humility and professional will."[68] He gives example after example of failures by vigorous leaders who sought to transform an organization by following a clear and compelling vision and insisting on adhering to clear performance standards. The successful leader is a modest person, often likable and, above all, a committed professional who has often been with the organization for a long period of time.

---

[68] Collins, Jim, Good to Great: Why Some Companies Make the Leap and Others Don't. New York: Harpers, 2001, p. 20.

It is possible for an organization to embrace technology and the work culture transformation that accompanies it. Embracing technologies and innovation, provides the possibility for a transformation in the work culture. Technology is an enabler of transformation, but it is not, in itself, a transformation.

The work culture of knowledge work is an information sharing, not an information hoarding work culture. The information hoarding work culture, which underpins the industrial mode of production, treats information as property and power to be protected and kept away from others. To share threatens the very essence of the established work process.

The efficiencies come through collaboration within communities, between communities, and among communities. The sharing of information, essential for knowledge work, makes that work and the work processes associated with the work more efficient and effective. Information sharing is not just a nice idea, not just a moral imperative, but is a better way to do work – when the work is knowledge work.

Creating a new work environment is, itself, work. In order for the work of transformation to be done effectively and efficiently, change must come from below, from the work place. Transformation is enabled through effective leadership, but the call to transformation must be accepted – one person or group at a time ... One way to describe the leadership necessary to transform the work culture is described in the appendix:

> *"You can't change culture using any process based on central control or hierarchical authority. There is no one individual or even collection of individuals within our system who have enough control or authority over enough of the population to mandate cultural change. And if you can't mandate cultural change, it is pointless to try to build a plan in the conventional sense for doing so ... I would suggest that we need to approach this challenge by attacking and redefining the accepted norms of behavior that define the culture we have today.*
>
> *As we consider how to achieve this end, it will be useful to consider that bringing about ... cultural acceptance ... is a bit like religious evangelism. You can't mandate that people believe in God. The Spaniards attempted this once upon a time, and even under the threat of torture and death, they failed to render their population uniformly Christian. In other words, the way to bring about the cultural change needed to make (a new) generally accepted way of doing business ... is for each individual*

*in that population to make a decision to act in accordance with
the norms which define the (new) culture."*

This is, clearly, only one possible way to conceptualize how cultural
change comes about, but it captures the essential fact that cultural transformation, the change in the norms and commonsense that we bring to
our work place, happens one person at a time. Bringing about this change
requires leadership more than management.

The Transformation Steps

The transformation of the work culture to an information-sharing, collaborative culture, brings additional benefits as information is shared more
effectively and efficiently.

Business reengineering focuses on transforming work processes . . .
how work is done.

Work culture transformation focuses on changing the environment in
which work is done.

These steps need not be done in any particular order, but each of them
must be done in order to transform a work culture successfully. These
steps will, we hope, provide a way to think about the transformation we
described above.

Step I. Identify the Work and the Workflow.

Workflow is the sequence of tasks, or necessary steps, that comprise a
business process. To understand the workflow of an organization, it is
important to look at things from a process perspective, rather than from
an organizational perspective. In other words, it is not the particular office
that does work . . . there are processes that often cut across organizational units. Simply laying out the bureaucratic structure of the
organization will not give us the workflow.

It is possible for two groups to perform the same work, but have an
entirely different workflow. In other words, the way that any particular
group accomplishes its work may be very different, but the work may be
the same. Work is not about how you spend your time; it is about what,
if anything, you accomplish.

Accomplishment is measured in relationship to the mission of the organization in which you do that work. Improving work processes by
improving workflow and transforming the work culture can both increase
productivity. Done together the results can be dramatic.

Identifying work, work processes and workflow is the single most important step in changing the work culture.

As we saw, work is not just activity. It is a matter of moving walls. We identify work by looking at the purpose (mission) of the organization. An organization or business generally has particular purpose(s). Identifying these purposes leads us to the work of the organization. An organization or business may involve a number of different, interrelated communities of practice to accomplish its purposes. Work is what people do that fulfills the organization's purpose. Work is meaningful activity stemming from and contributing to the mission of the organization. To answer the question "Is it a good idea to . . . ?"

Work is the "business" of an organization rather than the "busy-ness." In other words, it is the sum of the activities that cause an organization to accomplish its mission. Real work rarely consists of building briefings, preparing written reports, summarizing paper reports, meeting or traveling to coordinate work. Work is not just doing tasks, jobs, and other things that we do to spend the time at work to get a paycheck for a work week. Work, is what we do that makes a difference toward meeting the vision, the raison d'être of the enterprise. To know what this work is, we must know what the vision, mission, or reason for being is.

The first step is to identify the vision and mission of the business. Once you know that, you can identify what it takes to get there. That is the work of the company. Once the work is identified, then the processes involved in doing that particular work in this particular company can be defined.

The same work can be done in many different ways. Within a community, how work is done can vary dramatically. There can be many different work processes to do the same work. Different businesses and organizations can do the same work in very different ways, i.e. using different work processes.

We need to determine the real work (the sets of business activities that make up that work) as it is done in a particular situation.

Optimizing workflow removes non-value-added tasks from the work process. Workflow may be different from organization to organization – even if all organizations are all doing the same work. Optimizing workflow (the way we do work) allows us to leverage advancing information technology in to the business practice.

For example, every bank processes checks differently. The procedures, the software and the tools used to accomplish the work can be quite different. The workflow – how tasks are done – can vary from place to place. But the work of processing a check and passing the information from one bank to another requires an agreement on standard ways to communicate.

Similarly, different groups can do knowledge work very differently. It is not necessary to mandate HOW work is done. Freeing up work so that different people can do it differently enables a community to determine which work processes are most efficient. There need not be only one best way to do work.

How do I do a work process analysis – How do I analyze the work and the work processes?

Conducting a work process analysis requires perspective, objectivity, and an understanding of the business. Ideally, a team comprised of "objective outsiders", as well as, "intimate insiders" conduct the work process analysis. This analysis must be conducted within the framework of the business information enterprise. One way to identify work process is to determine what information you need from others and what information you provide to others. By identifying information products and needs, you can often identify work processes.

Define the Framework

First, you must understand business as well as the purpose of the process you are analyzing.

Then it is important to identify goals, objectives, and purpose of the work. What is the problem to be solved? (Increase productivity, reduce cost, reduce cycle time, improve quality, improve timeliness of reporting etc.)?

Finally the scope of work needs to be defined. From the practical sense, you will need to establish some boundaries as to what you will be addressing. This will help to keep the analysis on track.

Capture the as-is process

The capturing of AS-IS processes is good for two reasons:

1) To determine what is problematic about the current process, and
2) To determine the invariants in the process.

Invariants are items in the current process that cannot be changed from your vantage point. These include political constraints, facility constraints, and other issues outside your span of control. Invariants will be included in the new process, and must be planned for accordingly, unless you can somehow increase your span of control to change them.

Then it is important to look at the work process from the users' perspective (normally the customer or people who use the knowledge or other products that are made).

Identify what initiates the various business process. Is it a phone call to the help desk? Is there a cyclical pattern? These processes may indicate what the work is.

Identify the resources that affect your process. These can be money, time, manpower, information systems, information, etc. A model or chart representing the current work processes can serve as a common reference to communicate and come to a mutual understanding of the work process.

Once you have identified the real work (as opposed to the activities) and the work processes that are used by an organization to do that work, you can begin to take the necessary steps to transform the way you do work.

Even the most perfunctory work analysis reveals that much of what people do when they are "at work" is not work at all.

This is not because people are lazy or avoid work, but because many work tasks and processes were developed to meet the needs of an industrial mode of production, not the work itself.

As we noted earlier, those who have conducted many work analyses report that only twenty to thirty percent of the tasks done in a work place typically generate productive work – even in the best-run organizations.

Work analysis and the resulting re-engineering of work processes often bring substantial increases in productivity. But the real efficiencies come when new, more appropriate work processes develop in an integrated digital environment that spawns a new work culture.

The knowledge age requires a different kind of work and workflow and a work culture to go with it. It requires a culture based on the instantaneous access to information needed to do work. The second step in bringing about the new work culture is identifying information used to do the work and make it immediately accessible to those who need it.

Step II: Identify knowledge/information produced doing the work and make it it accessible to those who need it to do their work.

After determining the real work of the organization and how we do that work (our work processes), we then identify the knowledge that is created in the work and we begin to make it accessible to others.

Now we start to change the way we do our work. We begin to develop new work processes – processes based on very different assumptions than those we once had.

Instead of hoarding our knowledge (typical of linear work in an industrial world), we deliberately and openly make the knowledge created (which is information for others) accessible to those who need it for their work. We reach out to our customers – the users of our knowledge/information. We open up. The sharing of our knowledge as information to those who need it for their work that forms part of the collaborative relationship within and between communities. We do this not just because we are good people, but also because that is what it takes to do our real work productively and well.

This is not always an easy change to make, for there are many who believe that their positions depend on keeping information to themselves. Middle level managers are, to a large extent, primarily information collectors and disseminators, so making information immediately accessible to those who need it to do their work will be impeded by those who exercise great political power in the day-to-day operations of an organization.

Making the product of our work immediately accessible to others can feel a bit risky. We are used to dealing with scarce resources. If I give you some money, I have less and you have more. With knowledge/information, something very different happens – a new dynamic takes over. In the process of collaborating, new ideas occur, new solutions appear because two or more people are now considering the same information, and new products are born. Creativity enters the picture. The more minds that we apply to using the same information the more likely it is that something new will emerge.

As I make my knowledge accessible to my customers, I still have my knowledge . . . and the customers have more information now than they had before. I know more and my customers have more information. It is, as they say, a win-win situation.

This attitude/belief/work culture flies in the face of some of our most widely held beliefs. We think, for example, "knowledge is power" – and indeed knowledge can be very powerful. But knowledge is more powerful if it is shared in the collaborative process . . . and the more it is shared,

> The work products of knowledge workers should be stored and developed in such a way that the customers of the community can immediately access it:
>
> - The owner/creator is the keeper of information.
> - Do not copy anything.
> - Do not "uploat" to a common source.
> - Do work in the web and on the web.

the more powerful it can be because it grows exponentially. It gains value by sharing. In fact, just knowing who uses the product of my knowledge work enhances my work – that is the essence of practice/praxis.

As sharing becomes a part of our work culture – the assumptions, beliefs, behaviors and attitudes that encompass and inform our work change – the culture itself changes.

With the new set of attitudes, the work culture transformation process is underway.

Step III: Identify information used (or needed) to do the work and make it immediately accessible to you and your colleagues.

Once the products of knowledge work are identified (remember, this is a spiral process and will need to be done again and again), we need to identify what information we need in order to do that work. That information is often the product of knowledge work done by others – within our community and in related communities.

Finding what information is needed to do the work and where that information may be located is the third step in the transformation process.

Part of the transformation process requires the identification of the information domains used in doing the knowledge work.

Each core business activity has associated information domains. The domains may intersect, overlap and relate to several communities.

The information domains used in doing work are often kept in some kind of structured form . . . such as databases of information or collections of material. Identifying which of this information is relevant and making the connection to the task at hand is the essence of work within a community. A list of information domains will include some that are very important and some that are used only once in a while. Part of identifying information domains is determining who owns that domain . . . i.e. who knows what they are doing . . . and how that information is stored or made available. Some information is tacit and must be made explicit in the process of doing knowledge work. Examples are databases, people, or books.

As a part of the process of identifying information that is needed to do the work of the organization, the source and "containers" of that information are also identified. The "who has it?" "Where is it?" and "how can I get it?" Questions are asked and answered.

Information is organized data – which may be contained in documents, databases, reports, or someone's head. Just as a community of knowledge workers makes knowledge that is information for others, so information is needed to make the knowledge of that community. There may be several related information domains that are accessed in the process of doing knowledge work.

In a digital world where communities of practice define the information, each community can access several (though probably not many) information domains.

The transformation requires an organization to support the changes in the work culture that allow for optimum knowledge work by:

• Adopting policies, procedures and reward structures that encourage collaboration
• Supporting and building communities of practice
• Making the person who creates knowledge responsible for keeping it accurate and up-to-date
• Replace reporting with access to information

A Work in Progress

Many organizations are already actively engaged in reengineering and restructuring their work place in order to optimize the technical (cyber) environment. The uneven development of technology will continue, both within organizations and among organizations.

That does not mean, however, that the work culture transformation cannot begin until an integrated digital environment is created. Neither does it mean that the process of creating an integrated digital environment must await the establishment of a new work culture.

The two processes – work culture transformation – and creating a new technical and working environment go hand in hand and support each other.

One of the most important tasks to create an integrated digital environment is developing and maintaining the information strategy of a community.

An information strategy is a process, not an event – a continuing process of setting and resetting direction.

An information strategy is done by business managers, assisted by technologists. It focuses on:

- Information content
- Common information
- What information should be common
- How we define common terms
- How we share information
- Information processes
- Information understood in the context of process

Change Agents

In order to achieve a work culture transformation, each community needs to have change agents responsible for the cultural change. These agents will take different forms depending on the history and culture of the organization. Who in the organization is the agent is not important. What is important is that the change agents come with the authority and power of the leadership of the organization.

The leadership is more than the person with the power and responsibility in the organization. The leadership consists of those people who can get things done – who can move the organization. In order to bring about a cultural change – and not just letting it happen "automatically" with all of the disorder that brings – the leadership needs to embrace the transformation and take on the task of changing their work – and their expectations of others.

The leadership needs to adopt the sixth value proposed by Marshal for a collaborative workplace:

> *"The success of the Collaborative Workplace is most likely to occur when we can move away from the view of responsibility and accountability as being a policing function grounded in a top-down approach to relationships. Instead, we must move toward a view that full responsibility and accountability*

are horizontal, shared, and grounded in our individual and collective integrity as adults and professionals." [69]

Those who assume responsibility to bring about the work culture transformation need to lead, rather than manage. The experience of business and government shows that transforming a work culture requires supportive and fully committed leadership from above. It requires the leadership, from the very top, to adopt new ways to do work and to demand the same from those responsible to them.

It requires commitment by those in charge to make the change happen, but commitment is not enough someone must be responsible for making the transformation.

The leader must be

- a champion not a director
- a leader not a manager
- an example, not a demagogue

In other words, leadership enables change. People change. Leading an organization to and through transformation can be important work.

There is No Road Map

Road maps mean different things to different people and to the same people at different times. It might mean

- A set of directions on how to get from one place to another
- A suggestion of where you are within a bigger context
- An indication of how you might get from one place to another

In this case a roadmap is a strategy to go from one way of doing work (as if we were in a paper environment) to doing work in an integrated digital environment.

One possible change agent is a leadership panel charged with work culture transformation.[70] Such a panel:

---

[69] Marshall, Edward M. Building Trust at the speed of Change: The Power of the Relationship-based Corporation. New York. American Management Association. 2000, p. 35.
[70] Such a panel is described in the appendix.

- Sees the whole picture
- Has an information strategy
- Encourages
- Identifies seams
- Coordinates
- Divides up targets
- Leads
- Knows what transformation efforts are underway
- Applies attention and resources

A Spiral Process

Transforming a work culture is not a pilot project – at least not in the sense that term is normally understood. You cannot "try out" culture change in one place and then replicate it in others, because the very act of "trying out" changes the situation unalterably – if there is real change. You cannot pick change up and move it to somewhere else, for change comes out of a community with a history and a tradition and becomes embedded in the norms of the community.

We can learn from others – and from ourselves – and make work culture transformation a part of our work. In the end, however, work culture transformation is something that happens to us, in fact, is often forced upon us by cataclysmic events . . . and in which we can participate. We can embrace that "happening" or try to ignore it or resist it. But the happening will happen never the less.

Neither is it completed "once and for all." The transformation continues as new sources of information are found and new uses for the knowledge produced come forward. The transformed work culture is itself open to change and transformation.

CHAPTER 10

One Person at a Time

Transforming a work culture is about changing one person at a time. Knowledge work is replacing menial labor in our society, but that does not mean that every ditch digger becomes a knowledge worker nor every sales clerk becomes customer and community focused. It also does not mean that every manager suddenly starts to lead and not direct.

For that reason, every one of us is faced with the question – How do I respond to this new kind of work? How do I change my assumptions – and we know that assumptions are the hardest of all to change.

There are people who know how to bring about cultural change . . . and far-reaching ones at that. They are not generally those who specialize in "change management" – which focuses on incremental and predictable change within an organization and a culture.

My colleague, Evie Lotze, convinced me that organizational transformation is not unlike personal transformation. She believes that fairy tales can show us what it can be like to transform ourselves. The first step is to "accept the call" – a kind of language that this back-slidden protestant finds a bit unnerving at first. However, as she understands the term, it is not a spiritual event, but an acceptance of a call to adventure – a change in the mind-set that enables us to face – and overcome – the catastrophic events of life.

In a companion book to this one, she examines and fleshes out the role and function of myth. She gives us, on the basis of her experience and wisdom gained working with and through cultural change with many different people, some "advice." But it is "advice" that is a little different than that generally given by consultants or advisors to organizations.

She says:

"Go to work and be a Hero – do the real work of moving the wall – the wall that confines the present work culture. By hero we mean, recognize that you are an ordinary person who has received the "Call to Adventure" – however inelegantly it was delivered. Accept the call; take the next step, realizing that you are embarking on unknown territory. As individuals and organizations, accepting the call begins the journey. It is dangerous, but if we have the right armor and swords and leave markers on the way, we might survive – and even return triumphant.

Cinderella through the death of her mother, Hansel and Gretel through abandonment in a deep and dangerous forest, Ulysses through the Trojan War, or Psyche being thrown out of her marriage were condemned to wander from one impossible task to another.

Modern heroes may launch their journeys in response to political oppression, revolution, or the loss of home or business.

If you are the recognized leader, prepare others for the journey as well as yourself. Frame the Journey for those who would join you: workers, co-leaders, colleagues, the business community. Write, speak, lead, set the example; this helps others equip themselves for the journey. Each of those affected by your leadership, in your company or in your world will undertake a similar journey of transformation, but be affected by it in their own unique ways. Let them know about the lack of sign-posts along the way in this strange land they are about to enter. Alert them to the existence of trials and on the way. Tell them to expect monsters and roadblocks in this wilderness. Give them permission to accept aid from unusual sources – sources they never credited in the past. Hold out the hope of the boon for those who will undertake the journey and stay in the process to its end. In other words, give them a larger perspective than that of chaos from which to view the process on which you are about to embark. In short, engage the community – remembering it was the community that saved the Kingdom for the Queen in Rumpelstilskin and rescued from obscurity and entrapment its new leadership.

Put yourself forward in time – far enough for the new work culture to be firmly established, for philosophers to be announcing that the Knowledge Age is about to give way to the next revolution.

At the end of the Knowledge Age, as yet another emerging age throws its shadow on the horizon, sages of the transformation process may look back and say, "here is the road map followed by those heroes who led the last transformation". Just as today, in retrospect, we can look back at the

Industrial Age and point to critical bends in the road and shifts in the culture that we now call the Industrial Revolution. Those caught up in the chaos of that transformation often went kicking and screaming into it.

Future philosophers and map makers may be able to say in their perfect wisdom: They took path 1, which led to road 2, they avoided the detour through the swamp en route to interstate 3 and so on to successful termination.

At this beginning point of the journey, we are still thinking a little, planning a little, deploying a little, learning a lot. However, even with our limited vision of the future, we can find ways to start our journey because we have a destination in mind. We know the potential that technology holds, we know the roadblocks the industrial culture throws up, and we know that the culture needs to be transformed. Furthermore, we know the stages of that transformation. The way might not be straight, we might have to go places for which we do not have a road map.

Besides, it is more fun to wander than follow a straight and narrow path – or at least it is a better adventure.

The uncharted territories, though, can be the most fun and rewarding ones of all for we will not only be Heroes but Discovers, Explorers and Adventures. Few are lucky enough to be an explorer, so bringing about a transformation in work culture can be fun, as well as rewarding (and a tad bit scary at times). We set off into uncharted territory with a map marked like the maps of old "Hic sunt animales" – Here lie monsters. The well-armed heroes of vision, like Christopher Columbus or the Vikings of old, will land on the shores of a New World.

The leader who would like to transform a work culture to one in which people achieve their highest potential and the company reaches its peak of productivity and profits has a daunting task. Other CEOs and managers may be tweaking the process, providing leadership training to promising new workers, assuring that change management techniques are widely known, and making sure his or her workers have all the latest bells and whistles. They may well be shaking their CEO-heads at our poor hero, thrown into the journey toward transformation; it is so "impossible to achieve." But in the end, it is the hero who returns with the boon, the benefit, the blessing. It is the hero who has a culture that supports collaboration in communities of practice; it is the triumphant returnee who has cut the Gordian[71] knot of compensation for knowledge workers who do not occupy an office or work regular 9–5 daily hours. It is the wanderer of wildernesses who has tapped the creativity of

---

[71] King Gordius of Phrygia tied a knot that could only be untied by the next ruler of Asia. Alexander the Great cut through it, solving the problem quickly and boldly.

colleagues and workers to design a system of work that works for all – for the company's profit and the workers' benefit. It will be the modern hero who has tapped the wellspring of development – and shifted the experience of the basis for reality in the work culture. Workers will bring to work a new set of expectations, a new "common sense" about how things get done; they will see reality differently."[72]

Accepting the Call

The "call" is not, however, necessarily a spiritual event, but is a dramatically different situation in which we find ourselves . . . . a situation that may occur for many different reasons. She calls it a "cosmic 2/4" that smacks us on the head – or other body parts – and gets our attention or, at least, gets us to curl up and try to escape the world.

I leave it to her to explore some of the ins and outs of the transformation process, but I have seen, working with her, that there is a kind of truth to what she says.

So, even though we may at times take the language of myth or tale, we are dealing with the nitty and the gritty of life – What do I do when I get up in the morning?"

We used to say, "I will go to work" unless we were on holiday and had made it through another work week to the week-end.

If work is no longer something that we "go to," then our daily lives will become much different. For many, this transformation is already underway. Men and women in all walks of life, of all ages, and in all countries, know they think for a living – and are embracing the new way of life. They are accepting the call to adventure.

Making a cultural change is more like "accepting a call" than it is "deciding to change." It is more like understanding that the world we live in is not under our total control . . . yet it is one that we can influence. We can, indeed, make a difference.

For knowledge work is about change . . . the transformation of information into knowledge. The work of culture change is a special kind of knowledge work . . . something that we can set out to do, even though we may not know the outcome when we start.

The environment required to do the work of changing a culture is the same environment that is needed to do all knowledge work. It requires trust. It requires courage. It requires armor.

---

[72] Lotz, Evie: Work Culture Transformation. Straw to Gold – The Modern Hero's Journey. Munich. Saur. 2004

Start Where You Are

You can start most anywhere, but in fact, we start where we are, for that is the only starting place there is. We need not wait for something else to happen before accepting the call to adventure . . . the new world we are entering.

There are no pre-conditions that must be in place in order to start to build an information sharing work culture.

What we can do, if we are in a position of leadership, is define and promote an environment that welcomes and promotes knowledge work, the work of changing information into knowledge. This environment is one in which every knowledge worker has immediate access to the information need to do work and makes the product of work available to others as information for their work.

In a previous chapter, we gave a three step "methodology" for transformation; a series of steps that can bring about that change. These methods come from the worlds of business process reengineering, quality improvement and change management. They can, and are, being implemented by organizations and leaders of organizations.

But what makes this methodology powerful is that it is not just a set of directions on how to build something, but embodies a vision of how things can be.

As we have said, leaders can lead from above, but change comes from below – one person at a time. The transformation of the profession into a job requires the knowledge worker to jettison a host of assumptions about the social place of the professionals. Professionals traditionally thought of themselves as self-employed, free-standing intellectuals, who were able to determine their work, their pay and how they used their time. To be professional was to get out of the world of work.

The so-called "menial" worker who becomes a knowledge worker can not only have more pride and ownership in the work place, but must also accept a new degree of responsibility. For really, no work is menial, if it is real work. And no worker should be treated as a menial person.

For in the end, and in the beginning (but not always in the middle), we can see clearly what it is that we are about: a work culture that enables us to share information. A work culture that enables us to do work. It is not so hard, but then it is not so easy either.

The Age of Knowledge can have a Happy Ending – full of surprises with richer and fuller lives for us all. But happy endings do not happen automatically . . . although endings – happy or not – are almost always full of surprises.

Appendix: The Air Force Project: From computers and wires to a culture change

By Terry Balven

(Terry Balven provides the context out of which many of the conclusions presented in this book were developed – a multi-year project to create an integrated digital environment for the Air Force, which concluded that a transformation in work culture from an information-hoarding to an information-sharing work culture is required to take full advantage of digital tools. Terry Balven was the Air Force Colonel in charge of the project. Ken Megill led the contractor team assigned to develop the project.)

When Al Gore was Vice-President of the United States (1993–2001), he played a major role as a proponent and sponsor of what was called "re-inventing government." One of the thrusts involved taking full advantage of technology to improve business practices. This particular theme was broadly embraced and resulted in a large number of initiatives that focused on the application of information technology in a variety of ways to "streamline" government operations.

Within the Department of Defense this manifested itself in a number of Defense Reform Initiatives built on a theme of moving to "digital" or "paper-free" processes. For their part, the acquisition community stepped up to this by deciding to build an integrated digital environment within which to manage acquisition and sustainment. At the level of a one paragraph description, the concept was clearly attractive though difficult to crisply define and impossible to create in anything like the term of a single administration.

While well intentioned, the resulting work constituted an array of essentially non-coordinated activities, each of which could produce automated systems or tools, many of which could produce improvements in performance of a process or activity, and few of which would contribute to the integration of the business environment.

Like many such initiatives, the proposal called for new actions beyond the scope of things currently being done by anyone in the existing organization. This was not simply a matter of doing more of what was currently being done (though much current activity was targeted at the same or related purposes). So, while the appropriate response to the proposal was debated, staffed, and fleshed out by government people at many levels, doing the new work would mean contractors hired to do that job.

Of course, such initiatives are always accompanied by pressure to demonstrate progress and results. That pressure is felt by people executing projects, but also by people in the chain of command between those executors and the senior leadership with grand expectations. One result of this pressure is the tendency to define and measure success in terms of things that can be built or bought and that can be scheduled and counted. While abstract purposes must always be converted into an understanding of what has to really be done to produce the desired capability, that conversion sometimes is not followed up by an assessment of whether the delivered things actually deliver the initially envisioned capability – an assessment that's often more qualitative than quantitative.

How it came about

The National Performance Review (NPR) proposed numerous initiatives on the use of technology to improve business practices. The approach built on the business process reengineering (BPR) movement that played an important part in industry and government in the early nineties.

In the Department of Defense, the NPR direction took the form of Defense Reform Initiatives (DRIs), many focused on moving to paper-free processes. In acquisition, this took the form of Office of the Secretary of Defense (OSD) direction to the Service Acquisition Executives to create an integrated digital environment. The focus of that direction was on individual program management offices (PMOs) or system program offices (SPOs – the term used by the Air Force for the organizations responsible for the management of a weapon system or a group of related programs).

The direction was passed to the various Services, each with its own tradition and its own way of solving problems.

The Army took the initiative as an opportunity to advocate for some substantial increases in funding for automation and advances in computerization. Within the Army, automation had proceeded at a slower pace. The Army was in the process of redefining itself and its future vision in terms of the digital battlefield, and the emphasis in the project was on the digitization in the "integrated digital environment."

The Navy, in its tradition, took the initiative as an opportunity to promote and develop a single, service-wide network. The thrust was on integration and controlling, from a central location, the flow of information and work. The Navy has long had to deal with far-flung operations executed by people needing to make decisions well within the cycle time of communications with higher headquarters. The Navy's counterpart to the Air Force image of the pilot (skilled, good-looking, and cocky) is the image of the ship's captain who is weeks sailing time away from his chain of command and needing to respond to the serious implications of a local incident. As technology makes better support to those people possible, we want to take advantage of it.

The Air Force, in keeping with its culture and tradition, emphasized the environmental aspects of the integrated digital environment. The work of the Air Force focuses on the people (stereotypically the pilot, but by extension every person on the team that operates or maintains a complex weapon system, such as an airplane). The importance of the person in the work is never doubted, within the Air Force tradition, despite those who claim that drones and rockets can replace a plane piloted by a skilled and trained professional. (The Air Force objection is less that drones aren't useful, but the concept seems to ignore the human element of making a drone available and productive.)

Several people have commented that they are surprised that the military would undertake such changes at all. The thinking is that the military's rigid, hierarchical approach is at odds with even thinking about such a new environment. The military has recognized for centuries the chaos and unpredictability within military operations (the fog and friction of war). The structure that it puts in place is an attempt to minimize those effects to the degree possible. The right balance between rigor and flexibility, better equips the organization and the individuals for the challenge. The individual platoon leader must make his own decisions, but will have a context within which he can judge his position and the likely actions of other platoon leaders also making their own decisions. When viewed in isolation (as in peacetime) the military structure can seem overly rigid. While that is an understandable misconception, the fact is that military people are bright, flexible, and innovative and see the need for constant adaptation.

The work of the Air Force has been digital for half a century. The Integrated Digital Environment Project was directed from the highest levels of the Acquisition and Sustainment part of headquarters. (In this context, sustainment is defined as the management of a weapon system that has been introduced into service. This is distinct from the management of the wholesale logistics processes that provide a supply system and depot maintenance capabilities, and from the operational logistics associated with the operation and maintenance of those weapon systems. In other words, it's the part the "System Program Office (SPO)" plays in the set of processes required to support the operational Air Force.)

The office in charge of the project (SAF/AQ) manages a $25 billion dollar budget each year that focuses on developing and producing weapon systems. It is also responsible for the systems engineering and management of those weapon systems for which the logistics community spends another $20 billion on maintenance and supply requirements.

This activity includes the largest research and development laboratories in the world, testing facilities, engineering enterprises, and contracting and financial activities to manage Air Force weapon systems. Though acquisition and logistics remain separate functions at Headquarters Air Force, system development and wholesale logistics were integrated into a single major command in the early 1990s. Within Air Force Materiel Command, the leadership of acquisition and sustainment activities has been aligned. In the Air Force, there is a firm commitment, still being worked out in practice, to see and implement development and sustainment as part of a single, coherent activity.

It is not surprising, therefore, that the Air Force part of the IDE project focused on the environment. The basic premise of the Air Force response to the original "Office of the Secretary of Defense (OSD)" direction was that the integration of SPO and contractor digital systems for individual program would not constitute the creation of an integrated digital environment. The Air Force argued that the real goal is not digital operations. The real goal is increased effectiveness and efficiency in the acquisition and sustainment community, reflected in: (1) better informed decision making, (2) reduced cycle times, and (3) increased productivity.

Unlike the other services, the Air Force contractors charged with developing the project were not from within the service.[1] They came with a fresh perspective which often challenged many of the assumptions –

---

[1] Ken Megill led the contractor team.

although the leadership of the team from within the Air Force was, throughout the project, in the hands of an experienced professional[2] rooted in the world of logistics who was familiar with the intricate decision-making procedures of the Pentagon.

The project went through four distinct phases:

Phase 1: 1998 – Identification of the problem and development of a strategy. The team, through a wide-ranging discussion with a large number of participants, defined an integrated digital environment as one in which information needed to do work is immediately accessible. From the beginning, the team emphasized that creating an integrated digital environment is not about wires and computers, but about how work is done.

Phase 2: 1999 – Identification of offices where local initiatives to establish an integrated digital environment were underway. Small teams visited a number of selected "System Program Offices (SPOs)" to identify how information sharing, process integration, and communication were being accomplished. (The approximately 100 SPOs effectively constitute individual "businesses", each headed by a Colonel [a few Generals head the most significant programs] with the authority to manage a business of anywhere from 50 to 500 employees with an annual budget in the hundreds of millions of dollars [but perhaps as much as $3 or 4 billion].) The team found that, almost without exception, those involved in leading-edge automation projects identified the cultural impediments as their greatest hindrance to achieving an integrated digital environment. The team encouraged the development of innovation centers and called them together for a symposium in Seattle, Washington in September 2000.

As a result of the work done during this phase, the team identified three principles of an integrated digital environment:

- The owner/creator of information is its keeper,
- Reporting replaces access, and
- Essential evidence is preserved for re-use in the organization.

Phase 3: 2000 – Introduction of principles. The three principles were introduced, with varying success, and tested in innovation centers. The most successful principle, replacing reporting with access, was particularly welcomed. This principle flies directly in the face the of the traditional working relationships of an hierarchically organized military – where information is fed up through a chain of command through reports, generally in the form of briefings, to increasingly higher levels. The leadership makes

---

[2] Terry Balven was a career Air Force Officer.

decisions on the basis of information contained in these reports. A number of different offices embraced the principle that immediate access to information should replace reporting . . . and that the leadership should be able to "look over the shoulder" of those doing the work in order to get the most up-to-date information that is available. The other two principles were also, in varying ways, carried out.

Phase 4: 2001 – The project concluded with the establishment of a Work Culture Transformation Board formally established by the Assistant Secretary of the Air Force to "make use of the knowledge and experience gained by the Air Force integrated digital project as applied to the acquisition and sustainment community." The envisioned transformation of work and work culture will require: (1) changes in business processes, (2) investments in information technology as enablers, and (3) a different mental model about how work is done. While all these are essential components, the culture change was recognized as the most difficult part – and the one deserving the most attention. This is, in part, because it is the least likely to be properly addressed (if at all, as most projects move quickly to process redesign and tool development).

With the creation of the Board, the external project team withdrew its participation. Since that time, despite the increasing strains that come from more active warfighting, the commitment to work culture transformation remains. A change in administration came in 2001 with an increased emphasis on transformation. The integrated digital environment proposal was started under the Clinton administration, but it dovetailed with many of the sentiments of Secretary of Defense Rumsfeld. In his confirmation hearings he emphasized, "The legacy of obsolete institutional structures and processes and organizations does not merely create unnecessary cost. We are in a sense disarming or 'under-arming' by our failure to reform the acquisition process and to shed unneeded organization and facilities."

The Role of Leadership

It is perhaps not surprising that a discussion of the role of leadership in cultural change occupied a great deal of time and energy in a project for the Air Force. Military organizations rely on leadership to bring about change. They are structured to achieve specific goals when called upon. As one observer said, the work of the military is to wait and be prepared. Once called upon, leadership is needed to mobilize and move people.

A view of leadership is contained in a paper written by one of the participants in the project, Colonel (ret) Andy Nodine shared his views on how a cultural change comes about in the following piece that he wrote as a participant in a symposium as a part of the project.

"My basic premise is that you can't build a plan in the conventional sense (i.e., a progression of tasks and milestones with dates connected to them) for cultural change. And my concern . . . and motivation for writing this piece . . . is that, if we go into this conference thinking that this is our objective and believing that it is achievable, all we are going to wind up with is frustration.

Here is my rationale:

Let me begin by positing a definition for the term "culture."

I would suggest that culture is the corporate behavior pattern that emerges among a population based on the decisions made independently and autonomously by the individual members of that population about how they choose to behave.

I would further suggest that these individuals generally make their decisions about how they are going to behave based on certain widely accepted norms of behavior and conceptions of self interest, which can often be identified and defined as the essence of the culture.

If we accept this definition, then it should be obvious on the surface that you can't change culture using any process based on central control or hierarchical authority. There is no one individual or even collection of individuals within our system who have enough control or authority over enough of the population to mandate cultural change. And if you can't mandate cultural change, it is pointless to try to build a plan in the conventional sense for doing so.

That said, then how are we to approach the challenge of bringing about the cultural change needed to make IDE an accepted norm of behavior?

I would suggest that we need to approach this challenge by attacking and redefining the accepted norms of behavior that define the culture we have today.

As we consider how to achieve this end, it will be useful to consider that bringing about the cultural acceptance of IDE is a bit like religious evangelism. You can't mandate that people believe in God. The Spaniards attempted this once upon a time, and even under the threat of torture and death, they failed to render their population uniformly Christian. The decision to become a Christian is made only by individual people as they choose to accept the tenets of this faith. But once an individual has become a Christian, they generally comply with the set of behavioral norms expressed in the Bible. Accordingly, the only way to make Christian behavioral norms the norms of the society as a whole is to individually convert each soul in the population.

In other words, the way to bring about the cultural change needed to make IDE the generally accepted way of doing business in the Air Force is for each individual in that population to make a decision to act in accordance with the norms which define the IDE culture."

And if that is the case, then I would further suggest that the best possible outcome of this conference would be a consensus among all of the attendees concerning a new set of behavioral norms. A second outcome would be a commitment from each of them to behave in accordance with those norms and to influence all those within their spheres to do likewise. Of course, it would also make sense for us to do what we can to create incentives for ourselves and everyone else in the population of concern to behave as we would like them to.

Accordingly, I would suggest that our specific purposes at this conference should be to:

Define the attributes an IDE-based culture should exhibit,

Define the behavioral norms which, when complied with by the members of the population, will bring about that culture,

Obtain a commitment from each conference participant to behave in accordance with those norms and to influence those around them to "Go and do likewise," and finally,

Where possible, create incentives for ourselves, and those around us, to choose to behave in the desired manner.

It is my hope that this view of our challenge will enable us to define useful and achievable goals and to make real progress toward their accomplishment. As "fuzzy" as this approach may seem, I really do believe that this is the most direct route feasible toward bringing about the cultural change that is our ultimate objective."

Two points deserve to be emphasized. First, we can't directly change culture, but we can change behavior. We need to focus on desired behaviors and work to have people behave in that way – finding ways to encourage, facilitate, and incite the change. Only after behavior changes will people begin to internalize an adjusted set of values (the unwritten rules) that would ultimately be recognized as culture change. Second, good citizenship requires not just service, but leadership. While we all recognize the importance of the people we think of as great leaders, we are often content with "following" and "doing our part." But that's not enough – change can't happen without leadership. We all need to provide leadership, it's part of our responsibility to each other for the environment within which we live and work.

Glossary

If there is one thing that embodies a culture – it is a language. Language lets us communicate and the more similar our language is, the better we (generally) communicate. In this book, we use several terms in a particular way.

We hope that the Glossary will help the reader understand how we use some key terms and give us a common language to foster our communication. This glossary is not an attempt to give "standard" definitions, but as a help to the reader to know what the author has in mind when he uses a particular term.

Abduction – A form of logic identified by the American philosopher Charles Sanders Peirce to describe the process of creating knowledge. Abduction is the process of reasoning and work that puts assumptions and presumptions to the test by looking at empirical reality with one eye toward finding a new truth and, in the process, supplanting the "old" truth.

Ba – A Japanese term used by Ikujiro Nonaka to describe the environment and culture in which work takes place. Ba is the context that makes a safe haven for creation of knowledge.

Community – Communities are groups of people who work for a common purpose within an organization or across organizational boundaries. A community, traditionally, is understood, has a shared place or geography, a characteristic which is not necessary for digital communities.

Collaboration – Working together with others with a high degree of inter-dependency and trust to achieve a common goal.

Community of Practice – One of the new terms that help us understand and conceptualize knowledge work. A community of practice is a group of people bound together by a common class of problems, common pursuit of solutions, and a store of common knowledge and understanding.

Cooperation – Working together side-by-side to do work in a manner determined by management.

Culture – A culture embraces the common understandings, language and ways of acting and other assumptions shared by a community. A work culture is the "common sense" that pervades the work place.

Data – Data are the "facts" or raw material that makes up information.

Faceting – Faceting is a way of describing information developed by the Indian theoretician and practitioner Ranganathan that focuses on the various ways in which information may be viewed, depending on its possible uses. Faceting focuses on uses and potential uses and the context information will be used, rather than the content of an information container, such as a book or article.

Hermeneutics (Theory of Understanding) – Hermeneutics is the methodology to interpret texts, particularly sacred texts. It has been expanded to be a methodology and theory of understanding by the German philosopher Hans Gadamer.

Industrial Age – The industrial "revolution" came when machines began to drive the productive process. Manufacturing brought workers together in large factories. With the steam engine and other machines (including computers) production began to be driven by the machines and the needs of the machines. A new kind of work took place based on cooperation.

Information – Information is processed data – it is the building blocks used by people when they create knowledge. Information generally requires data to be managed and processed – just as knowledge requires information to be managed and processed. But managing data and information are not identical.

Information Management – Information management is concerned with the acquisition, documentation, arrangement, storage, retrieval and use of information.

Integrated Digital Environment – An integrated digital environment is a work environment in which there is immediate access to the information needed to conduct business (to do work). Such an environment requires an information-sharing work culture, digital tools, connectivity, and corporate memory.

Knowledge – The traditional philosophical definition of knowledge is that it is justified true belief. Davenport and Prusak, two developers of knowledge management define it as"A fluid mix of framed experience, values, contextual information, and expert insight that provides a framework for evaluating and incorporating new experiences and information."[71]

Knowledge Age – The "fourth wave" – The age of work in which the production of knowledge is the chief productive activity. The Age of Knowledge follows the Information Age, which is the final stage of the Industrial Age, the Manufacturing Age, and the Agricultural Age. How we name the ages is not as important as recognizing a fundamentally different way of doing work is becoming a reality.

Knowledge Management – A methodology for making comprehensive, relevant information (current or historical) available in a timely manner for users (knowledge workers) to make timely valid decisions that increase the productivity of a business application (where a business application is a set of work processes).

Knowledge Manager – A knowledge manager is someone knows who the experts (knowledgeable people) are, and how to access their knowledge. A knowledge manager is not the same as an expert. An expert functions within a community. An expert is recognized as the one who "knows" more than other people do about a particular topic. An expert is the creator and developer of knowledge. A knowledge manager knows who the experts are and how to access their knowledge.

---

[71] Thomas H. Davenport, Thomas H. and Lawrence Prusak, Working Knowledge (Boston. Harvard Business School Press, 1998) p. 5.

Knowledge Marshalling – A term used by Colonel Roc Myers to describe the process of gathering knowledge together for a purpose and delivering it to those who need it.

Learning Organization – A term developed and popularized by Peter Senge and widely used in the knowledge management world to emphasize that an organization needs to have learning imbued into its culture. Learning should be centered on performance and done in the work place – not through training which takes people away from work into a class.

Manufacturing Age – Factories brought people together to do work which was once done at home or in small shops. By bringing workers into an urbanized environment, great efficiencies were gained by controlling and disciplining the work place and dividing the labor. Work, in a factory before industrialization (when machinery began to change the nature of work), was still done in the same way as before, only now under the discipline of a foreman.

Praxis (Practice) – Germans use "praxis" for the "business" lawyers and doctors maintain; it comprehends all their clients and all the work they do for their clients. Praxis includes more than the English verb to practice, it includes customs and cultural content, as well. Praxis is often translated as "practice" in English, but it comes with very different overtones. Praxis implies a combination of theory and action.

Rationalize – The application of "scientific" principles to work. This rationalization is the basis for the industrial mode of production where automation replaces physical labor. Work is divided into pieces and each piece is made as "rational" (efficient) as possible. Management oversees and coordinates the process.

Spiral Development – A methodology first developed and used to make software but now widely applied to other activities that accepts the fact that we cannot plan and lay out exactly where we are going and need to work in spirals.

Standards and Connectivity – A decision by a community to conduct business in a certain way. Standards arise, normally, when it is necessary to communicate. Standards do not, however, mean standardization. There is no need for everyone to do things in the same way, as long as they can communicate.

Systems Thinking – A methodology developed by systems theorists that emphasizes the importance of looking at actions within the context, rather than isolated activities.

Transformation – Transformation is a change that is profound enough to cause a change in the physical, mental, or cultural form of the object or institution.

Understanding – Understanding takes place within a context – out of a history and community. Understanding contrasts with explanation which is ahistorical in nature.

Work – Work is Force times Distance. It is production, not just activity. Work focuses on those activities that lead to an organization accomplishing its mission. Work is organized through tasks that are linked together in an application – a set of related work activities.

Work Culture – Work Culture is the environment in which Work is done. It encompasses the attitudes, beliefs and presuppositions that we bring to our work.

Work Culture Transformation – A transformation of the work culture is evidenced by observed and qualitatively measurable change in behavior – from an information hoarding to an information-sharing environment.

Workflow – The sequence of tasks, or necessary steps that comprises a business process. Two groups may perform the same Work, but use entirely different work processes or workflow. Optimizing workflow removes non-value-added tasks from the work process in order to improve productivity.

Work Process – Work Processes are comprised of a series of tasks to deliver value to a customer. It is not a department (e.g., Accounts Receivable), nor is it simply a collection of activities or tasks. The tasks must be held together by a mission: delivering value to a customer.

Work Tasks – Specific activities which when combined form the work process.

For Further Information

Alberts, David S., et al, Network Centric Warfare: Developing and Leveraging Information Superiority. Washington DC: National defense University Press, 1999. Available on-line at http:///www.dodccrp.org.

Full of jargon decipherable only to those embedded in the discussion of military tactics. If you wade through the words, however, you find an insightful and thought provoking book on knowledge management.

Apel, Karl-Otto. Understanding and Explanation: A transcendental-Pragmatic Perspective. Translated by Georgia Warnke, Cambridge, Mass, MIT Press, 1984.

Originally published in 1979, this book describes the distinction between understanding and explanation. Not a quick read, but for those who persevere, lots of insights. The author was a student of Professor Apel when they were both young men (in 1961). Many of the ideas in this book come from Apel, who introduced the author to Gadamer and Peirce (as well as Heidegger and a range of other philosophers).

Gadamer, Hans Georg. Truth and Method (Wahrheit und Methode). 2nd revised edition. New York. Crossroad. 1989.

An epoch-making exposition of the theory of hermeneutics, the theory of understanding.

Baumand, Philippe. Tacit Knowledge in Organizations. (Organisations déconcertées) Translated by Samantha Wauchope. London. Sage Publications. 1999.

Much of the best theoretical work in knowledge management comes from Europe. This translation of a French book focuses on the nature of knowledge in an organization that is not explicit. The book develops a theory for tacit knowledge and then tests the theory through four very different organizations: Quantis, the Australian Airline, Indigo, a publishing company selling information through specialized confidential newsletters; Indosuez, a bank operation in international finance, and Pechinery, an aluminum production company active in Guinea.

Boudieu, Pierre. Practical Reason. On the Theory of Action. Politc. 1998 (translation of French book published in 1994.

Chapter 2, "The New Capital" is a particularly interesting discussion of the production of cultural capital.

Chaiklin, Seth and Lave, Jean (ed) Understanding Practice. Perspectives on Activity and Context. Cambridge University Press. 1993.

A collection of articles on the nature of practice and work from various specific perspectives. The essay by C. Keller and J.D. Keller, "Thinking and Acting with Iron" describes the work of a black smith in terms of "what it is one needs to know or believe in order to behave appropriately." "Rather than an exclusive focus on either the mental or the material, we have focused on the inherent integration of internal representations and external objects in accomplishment of a task . . . . One needs, therefore, to know enough directly or indirectly to conceptualize an orientation toward a goal: to provide combinatorial arrangement of previous knowledge in the service of new, and therefore partially unknown, production . . . All one needs to know is really only specifiable on the attainment of a goal."

Collins, James C. Good to Great: Why Some Companies Make the Leap – and Others Don't. New York: Harper Business. 2001.

A brilliant report on statistical and empirical research done of great companies to identify what distinguishes them from good companies, defined purely in terms of stock values over a fifteen year period. The research debunks many notions of what makes good change possible. His research team concludes that leaders of great organizations (as contrasted with good ones) generally come from within the organization and are shy, modest and focused in their work. They are not the "charismatic" leader put forward by many change theories. The salary paid to leaders in a corporation has little correlation to success. He urges companies to preserve core values and core purposes while changing culture and operating practices (p. 196). He emphasizes that effective transformation is organic in nature.

Davenport, Thomas H. Process Innovation: Reengineering Work Through Information Technology. Boston, Mass: Harvard Business School Press, 1993.

One of the better and most influential descriptions of business reengineering. Davenport's work is particularly good because he has a sound understanding of the role and function of information and knowledge and how technology is transforming work.

Dierkes, Meinolf (ed), Handbook of Organizational Learning and Knowledge. Oxford: Oxford University Press, 2001.

A hefty compendium of nearly a thousand pages of articles by the leading contributors to the development of a theory of learning as a part of knowledge management. A valuable resource that attempts to identify the "state of the art" in the field of knowledge management.

Dixon, Nancy M. Common Knowledge. How Companies Thrive by Sharing what they Know. Harvard Business School Press. 2000

A description of the process of knowledge transfer in large businesses. Specific examples are given how businesses have learned to transfer different types of knowledge from one place to another. The emphasis is on the interrelationship of people and tools (databases, etc) that enable knowledge to be shared.

Dixon, Nancy M. The Organizational Learning Cycle: How We Can Learn Collectively. Brookfield, VT: Gower. 1999.

Practical advice for working within and fostering a learning organization. Begins with the assumption that "it is certain that the Knowledge Age is here."

Harvard Business Review on Knowledge Management.

An early collection of articles published in the Harvard Business Review on knowledge management. Two are particularly noteworthy – Peter Drucker, "The Coming New Organization" and Ikujiro Nonaka, "The Knowledge-Creating Company." Drucker gives one of the earliest, and most influential, versions of the nature of knowledge work. Nonaka states the themes that appear in his many other articles.

Gavin, David A. Learning in Action. A guide to Putting the Learning Organization to Work. Harvard Business School Press. 2000

A good, solid book that goes beyond the earlier work by Senge and Nonaka. "A learning organization is an organization skill at creating, acquiring, interpreting, transferring, and retaining knowledge, and at purposefully modifying its behavior to reflect new knowledge and insights." (p. 11). He comments on Senge and Nonaka, "while uplifting, lack a framework for action and thus provide little comfort to practical minded managers." (p. 5).

Hagel, John. Net Gain: Expanding Markets Through Virtual Communities. Boston: Harvard Business School Press, 1997.

Infused with an unbounding faith that technology will solve all of our problems. It does give us some interesting ways to think about the nature of communities in a digital age

Hammer, Michael and Champy, James. Reengineering the Corporation. Harper Business. 2001.

Originally published in 1993, this classic book popularized the notion that a new kind of work is emerging. Chapter 4, "The New World of Work: describes the reengineering that "entails the radical redesign of a company's business processes . . . Jobs evolve from narrow and track-oriented to multidimensional. People who once did as they were instructed now make choices on their own instead." (p. 18)

Holland, Dorothy and Lave, Jean (editors). History in Person: Enduring Struggles, Contentious Practice, Intimate Identities, Santa Fe, NM, School of American Research Press Oxford: James Currey, 2001.

A thoroughly charming description of culture and cultural development from a variety of perspectives. My favorite is Lave's "Getting to be British," a description of the British colony living in Porto, Portugal. Shows the richness of culture and its pervasive influence in the way we live our lives.

Johnson, Spencer. Who Moved My Cheese?: An Amazing Way to deal with Change in your Work and in your Life. New York: Putnam, 1998.

A brilliant little tale of how mice and humans react to change. Enough lessons in this story to keep all of us thinking for a long time.

Kelly, Kevin. New Rules for the New Economy: 10 Radical Strategies for a Connected World. New York, Viking. 1998

Clever slogans describing the new work culture. The assumption underlying the "new rules" is that the technological advance is the sole driver of organizational change. But the "new rules" do help articulate the collaborative and non-hierarchical working environment of the Knowledge Age.

Lave, Jean and Etienne Wenger, Situated Leaning. Legitimate Peripheral Participation. Cambridge: Cambridge University Press, 1991.

A brilliant little book by two people who went on to provide much of what is good in knowledge management theory today. The book shows that the best learning is "peripheral" – in a situation. The final chapter introduces the term community of practice.

Lave, Jean and Wenger, Etienne. Situated Learning. Legitimate Peripheral Participation. Cambridge. 1991.

Shows how learning takes place in context – through the periphery. Apprenticeship is examined as a way to learn in a community of practice.

Lotze, Evie. Work Culture Transformation. Straw to Gold – The Modern Hero's Journey. Munich. Saur. 2004.

A companion book to this one written by a clinical psychologist who applies her knowledge of personal transformation to the world of organizational change.

Marshall, Edward M. Transforming the Way we Work: The Power of the Collaborative Workplace. American Management Association. 1995.

Marshall defines collaboration as "A principle-based process of working together, which produces trust, integrity, and breakthrough results by building true consensus, ownership, and alignment in all aspects of the organization." (p. 4) This is an excellent book that shows the power of collaboration from the viewpoint of management.

Nonaka, Ikujiro and Teece, David J. Managing Industrial Knowledge: Creation, Transfer and Utilization. London. SAGE. 2001.

One of several collections edited by Nonaka. Of particular interest is his description of "Ba" and Leadership – themes found in every one of his writings. The final chapter by Hirotaka Takenchi points toward a universal management concept of knowledge, drawing on the experience of the Japanese the Europeans and U.S. authors.

Ortega, Bob, In Sam We Trust. The Untold Story of Sam Walton and How Wal-Mart is Devouring America. Random House, 1998, p. 130.

Ortega gives a chatty biography of the founder and inventor of Wall-Mart. The biography draws heavily on Sam Walton's autobiography, but does recognize that not every human need is met by ruthlessly applying the profit motive.

Ranganathan, S. R. The Five Laws of Library Science. Bangalore: Saranda Ranganathan Endowment for Library Science: New Delhi. 1988.

A brilliant book full of wit and good advice for anyone who is entrusted with managing information and conveying knowledge. It is at once both practical and wise.

Rosenbloom, Richard S. and Spencer, William (ed). Engines of Innovation: U.S. Industrial Research at the End of an Era. Boston, Mass. Harvard Business School Press. 1996.

A collection of articles grappling with how industrial research and development is done in the United Statues. No answers are given to what the authors see as a serious problem in the way research and development is organized in an industrial setting. In the introduction they say, "The old assumptions about the proper conduct of research in industry will not hold in the era that lies ahead. The authors explore the dilemmas arising from this circumstance, finding no clear path toward resolving them." (p.7) Much of the fundamental research was once carried out in centralized research laboratories attached to and funded by major corporations such as Bell Labs (connectivity), DuPont (chemistry) and Xerox (document management). There is lots of attention paid to how work is organized, but none to the changing nature of knowledge work.

Senge, Peter M. The Fifth Discipline. The Art and Practice of the Learning Organization. New York: Doubleday/Currency, 1990.

The inventor and popularizer of the term "learning organization" – a powerful concept now part of the knowledge management field.

Stewart, Thomas Al. The Wealth of Knowledge: Intellectual Capital and the Twenty-first Century Organization. New York, Currency, 2001.

Focuses on the concept of intellectual capital – how to measure it and account for it,

St. Clair, Guy. Beyond Degrees. Professional Learning for Knowledge Services. Munich. Saur. 2003.

St Clair is on the forefront of those pushing librarians into the knowledge age. His latest book calls for the creation of a "knowledge services" profession.

Wenger, Etienne. Artificial Intelligence and Tutoring Systems. Computational and Cognitive approaches to the Communication of Knowledge. Morgan Kaufman. 1987.

A wonderful textbook – the beginning of Wenger's work. He suggests there are two types of knowledge: compiled and articulated. "Kitchner (1983) defines intellectual knowledge as the warranted belief, where the 'warrant' for a belief is a set of specific experiential episodes that have given rise to the belief that justify it to a particular person." (Kitcher, P. The Nature of Mathematical Knowledge. Oxford. 1983.

Wenger, Etienne. Communities of Practice: Learning, Meaning and Identity. Cambridge: Cambridge University Press, 1998.

The best book on communities of practice – readable, provocative, and thoughtful. Truly a groundbreaking work. His later books give practical advice on how to build communities of practice.

Wenger, Entienne, McDermott, Richard, Snyder William. Cultivating Communities of Practice: A Guide to Managing Knowledge. 2002.

A practical guide focusing on the creation, development and nurturing of communities fo practice.

Other books by Kenneth Megill

Corporate Memory. Records and Information Management in the Knowledge Age. 2nd edition. Munich. Saur. 2004

Document Management. New Technologies for the Information Services Manager (DM). London. Bowker-Saur. 1999.

Making the Information Revolution. A Handbook on Federal Information Resource Management. Silver Spring, MD: Association of Information and Image Management. 1995.

The New Democratic Theory. New York: Free Press. London: Collier-Macmillan. 1970

Index

K·G·Saur Verlag

Evie Lotze

Work Culture Transformation
Straw to Gold -
The Modern Hero's Journey

2004. X, 193 pages
Hardbound
€ 78.00
ISBN 3-598-11637-3

In the 21st century it is essential that information professionals adapt to a new way of working, ensuring their survival as a profession, but also ensuring that knowledge is used to its optimum within the work place.

This unique book approaches the problem in a totally new and imaginative way. It clearly demonstrates the need for change and most importantly ways to help individuals and organisations succeed in work culture transformation by using metaphors occurring in fairy stories, myths and fables. It is an excellent practical approach to a problem which torments managers.

This book is essential for any information manager dealing with change, large or small. It will be invaluable to all managers with the responsibility for providing an information service in the 21st century.

www.saur.de

K·G·Saur Verlag
A Part of The Thomson Corporation

Postfach 70 16 20 · 81316 München · Germany
Tel. +49 (0)89 769 02-300 · Fax +49 (0)89 769 02-150/ 250
e-mail: saur.info@thomson.com   http://www.saur.de